LOVE

Beyond

BORDERS

Secrets to a successful long-distance relationship

Blessing Oluwamayowa Ekundayo

Copyright © 2019 by **Blessing Oluwamayowa Ekundayo**

Love Beyond Borders: Secrets to a Successful Long-Distance Relationship

All rights reserved. No part of this publication may be reproduced in any form or by any means - graphic, electronic or mechanical including photocopying, recording, taping or information storage and retrieval systems without the prior written permission of the author.

Any person or organisation who commits any unauthorised copying of this publication may be liable to criminal prosecution and civil claims for damages.

This book is non-fiction. All the stories shared are real and permission granted by owners to share their stories. Some identities of the individuals have however been protected based on request.

Unless otherwise indicated, Bible quotations are taken from the New King James Version®. Copyright © 1982 by Thomas Nelson. Used by permission. All rights reserved.

Contents

Acknowledgements --- 5

Dedication --- 7

Foreword --- 8

Introduction -- 11

Chapter 1 -- 15

My Story --- 15

Chapter 2 -- 27

God First -- 27

Chapter 3 -- 35

You Next --- 35

Chapter 4 -- 53

Developing a Friendship -------------------------------------- 53

Chapter 5 -- 75

Be Accountable --- 75

Chapter 6 -- 83

Communicate Regularly -- 83

Chapter 7 --- 101

Trust Each Other -- 101

Chapter 8 --- 107

Do Things Together -- 107

Chapter 9 --- 123

Take Your Time -- 123

Chapter 10 -- 129

Long-Distance Relationship Love Stories---------------- 129

About the Author --- 157

Acknowledgements

I would like to thank God Almighty for the grace, wisdom and the wonderful idea He gave me to write this book. I really bless God for ordering the steps of my husband and I and for successfully seeing us through all the difficulties that were a part of our long-distance relationship. He proved to us that indeed, with Him nothing is impossible!

I also bless God for the lives of my parents, Rev. Dr. and Rev. Prof Mrs. Ezekiel Olatunde Agbaje, for bringing me up in the way of the Lord; for supporting my relationship and yielding to the leading of the Holy Spirit, even when it didn't appear to make any sense. If you both had been opposed to my relationship, I probably wouldn't be able to share my story today. I value and cherish you both greatly.

Thanks also to my lovely brother and sister for standing by me through it all. Olaoluwa and Folasade Agbaje, I love you both so much.

I am grateful to my parents-in-law for their words of encouragement and prayers throughout my relationship. I initially had a long-distance relationship with them too. Thank you for believing in me and supporting my husband and me on this journey. You are treasured by me.

To everyone who has contributed in one way or the other, those who willingly shared their stories with me to ensure others learn from the pitfalls of a long-distance relationship. I am very grateful. To Jack Minor who helped to proofread and edit my book, your effort is highly acknowledged and appreciated

Finally, but not least, I would like to thank my wonderful husband - Samuel Ekundayo; the man of my dreams, the man God brought my way to completely turn my life around for good. I am thankful that I walked this journey of faith with you. Thank you for trusting me totally, for loving me unconditionally, for working together with me and ensuring that we succeeded despite the hurdles. Thank you for inspiring me even on the project of writing this book. Your inputs to make my dream become a reality is greatly treasured. I love you with all my heart. God bless you.

DEDICATION

I dedicate this book to God Almighty, who inspired me to write. Also, to everyone in a long-distance relationship who is trusting God to make it a success.

I also dedicate this book to late Brother Kayode Amusan (my big brother) who played a very significant role in connecting my husband and I together.

Foreword

In this book, *Love Beyond Borders...Secrets to a Successful Long-Distance Relationship*, Dr. Blessing Ekundayo, one of those who found love beyond borders, has narrated her experience in a very simple and easily comprehensible manner. The material is therefore primarily a rich resource to assist others who may also find love beyond borders. The principles in this book are not only useful guides to the latter group, but also to others who seek to enter into a marital relationship, or even those who are already in one. They provide fundamental biblical guidelines that will be an aid to success in a marriage relationship.

Another great lesson taught by the author is to correct the notion that people who find love beyond borders can never yield any positive dividends. Dr. Ekundayo, in her write-up, showed that the problem encountered by some people in relationships and consequently in their marriages has little or nothing to do with the "how or where we met", but is more related to "our relationship with the Creator and Author of Marriage". Where the relationship of the persons with the Lord is sour, their experiences together will be non-palatable, even if they had met themselves physically. However, if they are both in tune with the Lord, they both will know how to receive guidance from Him through the inward witness by the Holy Spirit, and through the written Word of God. God's Word gives wisdom and prevents every obedient child of God from stumbling (Ps. 119:105). The Lord is the One who is able to lead a person through life without stumbling; even in the midst of storms, clouds, heights and depths, His unending grace is always more than able to see him through, provided the individual takes advantage of it.

Dear friend, you need not be scared of finding love beyond borders; your bother should be whether God is the One leading you or not!

This true testimony is a confirmation of God's faithfulness to everyone who puts his/her trust in Him. I would therefore recommend it for all singles, as well as all engaged and married couples.

Church workers and ministers will also find it useful for counselling their members.

Children of God, listen! This is the time for us all to win every satanic battle against homes. It started in the Garden of Eden and Satan has still not relented.

Join the winning team now!

Jesus is LORD!

MARANATHA!

Rev. Prof. Mrs. Esther Oluwatoyin Agbaje
Co-founder and Marriage Counsellor,
Christ's Charismatic Chapel International
Ogun-State, Nigeria

INTRODUCTION

Some people are of the opinion that long-distance relationships should never be pursued. Some pastors even preach against it as though it is a sin to be in a relationship with someone you are not in close proximity with. I came across a marriage counsellor on social media who said all the people she talked with who met via long-distance relationships went on to have problems in their marriage. To me, the idea that long-distance relationships have a 100 percent failure rate makes me marvel. I have a hard time accepting this! Very few things in life are an absolute sure thing, and this is even more true when it comes to something as complex as human relationships.

No relationship is free of challenges, whether long or short distance. It is true that a long-range relationship has its unique challenges, especially with regard to trust, so I can certainly understand the concerns of counsellors in this area. However, it is a known fact that trust issues frequently constitute a great challenge among all partners, including those dating in the traditional way.

Anecdotal evidence can be used to justify just about any claim a person wants to make. This is not to suggest we should dismiss these very real situations, but we should always be wary of substituting it for hard evidence collected using objective scientific methods of research.

This book is not intended to present such an analysis, either for or against long-distance relationships. Instead, for those who are in or are considering a long-range relationship, I would like to share my story about how I found love beyond borders. I will also deal frankly with the challenges my husband and I faced while we were in our long-range relationship and how we overcame them to have a happy marriage.

To God's glory, our long-distance relationship has resulted in six years of successful marriage at the time of the writing of this book with forever to go, and during that time God has blessed us with two wonderful boys.

I will also share stories from some others who found love beyond borders, and those who had to be separated by distance after finding love. You will find out how all of them made it through these difficult and challenging times.

By doing so, this will help you realize that even in cases where a long-distance relationship may not be the best option, it is still possible to succeed in it. You will also be reading from some of those who sadly did not succeed in long-distance relationships and learn the reasons why they failed.

By your reading and learning from their missteps, you will help ensure they receive a blessing through their being able to help others avoid the same mistakes and pitfalls they did. Although *Love Beyond Borders* takes you through the step by step process of finding love online, it can also be a useful book for those who initially found love offline but are now continuing their relationship as a long-distance one.

I hope that after reading this book, you will be properly guided and be able to guide others who may find love beyond borders.

Blessing Ekundayo

Chapter 1

My Story

"The steps of a good man are ordered by the LORD, and He delights in his way." (Ps. 37:23)

According to the MacMillan dictionary, a long-distance relationship is a romantic relationship between two people who live far apart and are frequently unable to see each other. In other words, it is an intimate relationship between partners who find themselves separated from each other geographically.

This was the experience of my husband and I before we got married.

I first met my husband online (hi5) in September 2007. I had just finished two years of Advanced Levels Programme and was waiting to gain admission into the university to study medicine. While at home for about five months, I found myself spending an excessive amount of time surfing the internet. Hi5 and Yahoo messenger were quite popular then.

I really enjoyed meeting people online and getting to know them. I always found it interesting to learn so much about someone I never met physically. I have established friendships with people from all over the world and I still keep in touch with many of them. During this time, I was not looking for love or a relationship; I just wanted a pure friendship that was strictly platonic.

In all honesty, I had made up my mind that I would hold off entering into a relationship until I began my final year of medical school.

I didn't want any distractions. I wanted to remain focused and succeed in medical school. Besides, I wanted to remain a virgin and desired to please God, so getting into a relationship too early might make me prone to falling into the temptation of fornication, which I did not want to do. I thought I had my life planned out, but God had better plans in store for me. Someone once said, "if you want to see if God has a sense of humour just tell him your plans for life."

"For my thoughts are not your thoughts, neither are your ways my ways, saith the LORD. For as the heavens are higher than the earth, so are my ways higher than your ways, and my thoughts than your thoughts". *(Is 55:8-9)*

I met my husband through one of my online friends who was also a Nigerian like myself but lived in Singapore. He was very cool but about ten years older than me. He really liked me and disclosed this to me, but the age difference was a barrier for me, not only that, he was ready to get married while I was wanting to wait at least another five years until I completed my degree. Knowing this, the two of us decided to remain very good friends. We talked very frequently (at least twice a week). I looked up to him as my big brother and he viewed me as his younger sister. He was the one who introduced me to his friend, who would become my future husband. One day, he told me he would like to introduce me to his "brother" who was living with him. I had no idea he had told his "brother" so many wonderful things about me, especially that I was a good girl and was smart. He also suggested his "brother" befriend me with the hope of getting into a serious relationship with me.

My big brother called me one day and we spoke over the phone. Then he passed the phone over to his "brother", who also spoke to me. We then exchanged pleasantries and he asked for my Yahoo messenger identity. We exchanged ids and then he told me his name – Samuel.

At this point, I would like to advise any single person reading this to be open minded and nice, especially with the opposite sex. You see, even though I was not interested in a relationship with my big brother, I was always kind to him, maintaining a platonic friendship with him. Our friendship was pure. I was not rude to him when he disclosed his intention of having a relationship. I just politely told him my goals and why I couldn't see us being together, which he understood and respected. It was this same man that God used to connect me to my husband.

To single ladies, realize that not all guys who come your way are right for you, but that doesn't mean they are bad people. It is important to maintain a good attitude in order to eventually meet Mr. Right, either online or offline. Some ladies have a very poor attitude and they reflect this whenever a guy approaches them for a relationship, especially if it is a guy who does not meet their "standards". I realize some guys can be annoying with their approach, but it is important that you remain polite and not be rude when turning down their proposals.

Some men are helpers of your destiny even if they are not your husband to be, but if you are too quick to judge and completely shut them out of your life with your bad attitude, you might have yourself to blame for the missing blessings they were able to provide. Examine yourself and make amends where needed.

The very first day I had a chat with Samuel, honestly, I was very disappointed in him. I am very particular about manners and etiquette, and find myself easily put off by poor manners. That day, I can't even re member what we were talking about. All I recall is that right in the middle of our chat he just logged out and left! I thought to myself, how rude! This guy is uncouth. How could he just leave a girl hanging?

I then caught myself and decided to give him the benefit of doubt, thinking perhaps there was a logical explanation like maybe the network was bad and he would quickly sign in again, or at least call me shortly to let me know what happened, but he never did. I did not call him either. That night when I laid on my bed to sleep, I heard the spirit of God whisper to me on the inside that Samuel was my husband. I just smiled and said to myself, ***This guy with a poor attitude?*** I replied back to God, saying that we would see how that would happen.

I never heard back from him until about a month later. The first thing I did was to challenge him about his behaviour and he immediately apologized. He explained that he was running late for work that day, which was why he had to log out quickly. Anyway, I forgave him, and we began finding out more about each other. From being acquaintances, we went on to become friends and eventually close friends. We chatted almost every day for at least two hours, despite the seven-hour time difference between Nigeria and Singapore.

We talked about our backgrounds, our parents, our individual future plans, our career plans, our likes, dislikes, values, love for God, knowledge of the Scriptures, our genotypes (Oh yes! I made sure I asked him early enough because I knew I was AC and had to marry a man who was AA to avoid conceiving a child who is SC and ultimately to avoid stories that touch the heart).

During one of our conversations, he began to share his past relationships with me. He was completely plain, open and brutally honest. You see, Samuel was not naive like me. He was well-experienced with relationships and was sincere with me, telling everything he had done. He felt that he needed to let me know that he was not a virgin like I was, but I was convinced that old things had passed away and he was a changed man.

I was already drawn to him because of his sincerity in this area because honesty attracts me. I knew I wasn't friends with a pretender, as he had an eventful past in the area of relationships. I felt that I could trust him. He was vulnerable enough to let me in on his past. He knew what he wanted from me and felt that I deserved to know in order to make my decision on him. On my own end, I had never been in a love relationship so I had nothing to share regarding this, but I had other pasts in my life before I completely gave my life to Christ that I was able to share with him. As we continued communicating daily, we soon realized how many things we had in common and became fond of each other.

In saying this, you don't have to share your past with someone if you don't feel comfortable about it yet or if you don't feel the time is right to do so. Samuel and I became very close friends and we felt very comfortable talking to each other about everything, including our pasts.

Do not feel compelled to do this if you are not ready to. However, anyone you are planning to commit to deserves to eventually know important areas of your past. It is not fair to hide this from them. For example, if you have a child from a previous relationship, it is not right to keep this from someone you intend to spend the rest of your life with. It would be unfair for them to marry you and then be surprised and devastated about such things. A relationship built on lies cannot stand the test of time.

If you are a lady, do not begin to tell every man who approaches you for a relationship about your virginity status. There must be a certain level of trust in your friendship before beginning to divulge such sensitive information. Meeting a guy online without first developing a friendship and knowing him well enough before sharing personal things about yourself or your past might make him interested in you for the wrong reasons or put him off before even getting to know you. This goes for both men and women.

A lady once got into a relationship with a man she met online. She had not known this guy very long and was quite naïve. He took advantage of her naivety and seduced her into sleeping with him. You need to be very careful before committing your life and heart to someone you met online. Do not be carried away by what the person says. Listen with your ears and open your heart, open your eyes, think things through before you "fall in love" so you don't get your heart broken.

Another lady asked me some time ago if she should enter into a relationship with a man who forced his ex-girlfriend to abort a pregnancy he was responsible for. She said this happened before he was born-again. I responded by asking about the status of his current relationship with God, if he had asked God for forgiveness for advocating the death of that baby and requested forgiveness from his ex-girlfriend, finding out what led to their break up. Finding out the answers to this question would give her some important insights into his personality, who he was, and whether he had changed or not. The Bible makes us to understand in Matthew 7:16a that "by their fruits, you shall know them." Be a fruit inspector to see if he has really changed.

I also made her to understand that if he really is a genuine and changed person, his past is behind him and God has forgiven him, so why should she hold onto that and not let go?

A person's past should not be a hindrance to being committed to them. However, if you cannot see beyond the person's past and see them the way God sees him/her, then I would suggest that you do not commit to a relationship with this individual.

Samuel was running his Master's Degree programme and planning to do his PhD outside of Singapore. We were both children of God, born again and Spirit filled. To God's glory, I gained admission to study medicine sometime in November 2007. Samuel was very excited about my admission. He knew becoming a doctor was my dream and promised to stand by me throughout the journey. In his words, "Treasure (as he fondly called me), we are on this medical journey together".

I had a strong feeling that he wanted more from me than just an ordinary friendship. He appeared to have fallen in love with me, and I sensed he was scared of losing me to the guys on campus, which he later confessed to me. After about six months of being very good friends and calling each other every day, he told me he intended to spend the rest of his life with me and I prayerfully considered his proposal (although it did not catch me by surprise). I said YES to him on the 14th of March 2008!

We officially began our long-distance relationship. It was a relationship of faith! We had no idea when we would see each other or what the future would bring. He could not afford the money to fly down to Nigeria from Singapore; he was still juggling being a student and a restaurant attendant, having just a small stipend to support himself and his family over there.

However, we were convinced that God was with us and we were confident that He would see us through. After almost three years of enjoying love beyond borders, we finally met each other for the first time in July 2010 and were married almost three years later on the 25th of May 2013!

At the time of writing this book, we have been married for six years and blessed with two boys, to God's glory.

"The LORD is good to those who wait for Him, to the soul who seeks Him". (Lam. 3:25)

How did we make our long-distance relationship a success? Did we have challenges? Find out in the following chapters.

Chapter 2

GOD FIRST

I am a Christian and I believe in God. I believe marriage was created by God, and to get marriage right you need to know the marriage Maker and work by the principles He has set forth for a successful marriage.

"Trust in the LORD with all your heart, and lean not on your own understanding; in all your ways acknowledge Him, and He shall direct your paths. Do not be wise in your own eyes; fear the LORD and depart from evil". (Prov. 3:5-7)

That being said, even though I was only 19 years old when I got into my first and only relationship, I never made any major life decisions without seeking God's face. I already had a relationship with God, which made things a lot easier. Remember how I mentioned in the previous chapter that the night after my first chat with Samuel, God whispered to me that this man was going to be my husband?

Dear reader, if you do not yet have a relationship with God, I would like to encourage you to start doing so now. Not just because you want to get it right in marriage, but most importantly, because having a relationship with Him is the only way to make Heaven your eternal home someday.

"…Most assuredly, I say to you, unless one is born again, he cannot see the Kingdom of God". (Jn. 3:3)

Realize that being a member or a worker in a church does not by itself mean you are a child of God. You can do the work of God without knowing and walking with the God of the work.

"Not everyone who says to Me, Lord, Lord, shall enter the Kingdom of heaven, but he who does the will of My Father in heaven. Many will say to Me in that day, 'Lord, Lord, have we not prophesied in Your name, cast out demons in Your name, and done many wonders in Your name?' and then I will declare to them, 'I never knew you; depart from Me, you who practice lawlessness"! (Matt. 7:21-23)

May that not be your portion; in Jesus' name. Amen.

A relationship with God makes your life so simple! Just like when you are on an aeroplane and place your life is in the hands of a pilot. You trust that he knows what he is doing and will get you to your destination safely.

Now, imagine going alone on a journey to an unknown place. That journey will be loaded with so much fear and uncertainty. You might have to seek help along the way from people to direct you. Sometimes, people end up misleading you. You are at risk of missing your way and wasting your time. On the other hand, if you find yourself in a vehicle with a driver who knows where you are headed, even if you have no idea how to get there, how do you feel? I bet you feel confident, being secure in his knowledge and expertise. Or if you are driving with the help of Google Maps, you are pretty sure you would get to the right place, although sometimes the app is not 100% accurate. A person with a consistent relationship with God is in the best company. You are sure not to miss it because His thoughts for you are thoughts of good and not of evil to give you an expected end (Jer. 29:11).

He knows our end, even from the beginning. He loves to guide His children in the right path. He wants to give us peace, He wants to give us that direction, that word, the peace we seek, whatever you want in your life and a relationship; if you have a relationship with God, it is a life made easy. This is my testimony and I would like to lead you to Him.

Before having an encounter with Jesus, who is the Son of God and God manifest in the flesh, my life was a mess. I was drowning in masturbation and lesbianism. I could hardly go a day without masturbating. I read all manners of erotic books to continue feeding my lustful and seductive desires. I had no time to concentrate on my studies in High School. No matter how hard I tried, I found myself going back to my vomit.

However, one day, I genuinely asked God to help me. I asked him to forgive me, I asked Him to come into my life and deliver me from the bondage of masturbation. I asked Him to take away those vile thoughts and fill me with His Spirit instead. I wanted to have control over this lust. I was tired of my poor grades in school because deep down, I knew I had the potential to be excellent. I knew I had the ability to excel (my father being a medical doctor, while my mother had a PhD, and my younger brother then was one of the best in his set). Unfortunately, I was one of the worst in my set.

My life changed when I met God. He came into my life and made me a completely brand-new person! I began to read my Bible rather than searching for erotic things to read. I began to spend more time praying, I cut myself off from friends who were a negative influence, I took my life very seriously. I stumbled a few times but refused to remain down. Whenever I fell down, I quickly got back up and went to God, asking Him for more grace.

"Let us therefore come boldly to the throne of grace, that we may obtain mercy and find grace to help in time of need". (Heb. 4:16)

I put time into my studies, causing my academics to take a drastic new turn. I began competing with the best students in my set and finished High School with distinctions! This earned me an admission into the university to study medicine at the prestigious College of Medicine, University of Lagos (CMUL). While on campus, I became the vice president of my fellowship – Christian Fellowship Group (CFG), where I had the opportunity to lead other people to Christ and encourage them to live for God.

It does not matter what you have done in the past or what you are currently going through. Abortion? Masturbation? Fornication? Lying? Stealing? Murder? How bad is all the wrong that you have committed? Maybe you are depressed and find yourself thinking that with everything you have gone through life is no longer worth living and you want to take your life.

Please hear me, God loves you and He wants the best for you. He has a great plan for your life.

"For God so loved the world that He gave His only begotten Son, that whoever believes in Him should not perish but have everlasting life". (Jn 3:16)

Don't let the devil continue keeping you in bondage! The Bible says that whosoever the son sets free is free indeed! Let God set you free completely. This was what He sent His son Jesus to die for, to give you peace and eternal life. Then to give you direct access to God 24/7, where you are now able to call Him your Father, to be able to speak to him about anything and everything, including your love life! He is able to guide you through every issue you face in life, big or small. Nothing is too big for God, and nothing is too small for Him either.

If you have not yet given your life to Christ genuinely, and you want Him to forgive you of all your sins, please, do not ignore this or delay because tomorrow might be too late. There are countless records of those who put it off until "later", only to discover they had lived the last day of their life. I would love to lead you to know God.

Please say these words sincerely: "Lord Jesus, I thank you for dying for me, I thank you for my life. I am sorry for all my sins and I ask that you forgive me. Come into my life and be my Lord and Saviour. Dear Lord, write my name in the Book of Life and help me to make Heaven my home someday. In Jesus' name. Amen".

Dear friend, welcome to my family. It is the family of God, the family of love with Jesus Christ as our elder Brother. I would like to advise you to find a Bible believing church and start attending it regularly where you can grow. The Bible describes you as being like a newborn baby. Just like an infant is completely dependent on others to feed and take care of him by giving him a diet of milk, you must get this spiritual nourishment if you ever hope to grow. You do not want to remain a child all your life.

Get a Bible devotional, study the Bible and pray every day. God is faithful; He sees your commitment, even if you don't do everything perfect or consistently. When you do these things, you will begin to hear Him speak to you, and you will be amazed at how simple and beautiful your life can be. Jesus loves you and I love you too.

Chapter 3

You Next

It is important for you to get your values right before getting into a serious relationship, especially a long-distance one. If you don't stand for something, you will fall for anything.

What do I mean by this? As a child of God, your values are determined by God's values in his word. His word is what we live by. The only way to truly abide by God's standards is to spend enough time with Him and His word. If you allow the Holy Spirit to renew your mind with His word, then His words will bear fruits in your life and your values will be attuned with His because you are His son/daughter.

"And do not be conformed to this world, but be transformed by the renewing of your mind, that you may prove what is that good and acceptable and perfect will of God". (Rom 12:2)

As a Christian single, one of the core values regarding relationships that must be clear in your mind is to understand that you must not under any circumstances marry an unbeliever. If you are unclear or doubtful in your mind regarding this particular counsel of God then you are not yet mature enough for a relationship/marriage.

Please remain single and don't complicate your life unnecessarily. The Bible makes it plain that Christians should not be unequally yoked together with unbelievers (2 Cor. 6:14b). An individual who has not been blessed to experience the genuine love of God, the unconditional love that only God can give cannot give you what he/she does not have! A person who does not share the same spiritual beliefs as you is a resounding NO! Do not get yourself entangled with such a person! This is not to say they are evil people, in fact they may very well be good and nice people, but you need to beware of this kind of relationship. The Bible says, "Can two walk together except they be agreed" (Amos 3:3). Understand this principle and abide by it before getting into any relationship. Compatibility in spiritual beliefs is key if you are to thrive. The spiritual controls the physical.

Both of you need to be in agreement spiritually; then you will be able to achieve the greatness and dominion that God has in store for you in marriage.

I believe one of the reasons for the success of my relationship was because Samuel and I were on similar frequencies spiritually. We were going in the same direction spiritually and this helped us tremendously.

If you become friends with the opposite sex online and this person begins to request nude or seductive pictures of you this is a giant red flag. It is clear that this person is only lusting after your body and does not really care for you or love you with a pure love. This person just wants your body to satisfy his/her sexual needs. Please, cut off such a person as fast as you can. Don't fall into that trap. Some have fallen into it, only to have their hearts broken online. It is clear that this person's values aren't in line with your values. Your nakedness is meant for your spouse only and not for a friend, not even your fiancé(e). Also, if they are bold enough to ask for these types of photos now, they will not hesitate to ask it of another woman after you are married because they have no concept of true love.

"My son, if sinners entice you, do not consent". (Prov. 1:10)

Other values a believer should have include honesty, humility, integrity, genuine love for people, respect, the list is endless. When you meet someone online and start having conversations with them, ensure you pay very close attention to the answers they give to your questions and don't forget them. Be sure to parse them to make sure they are not attempting to skirt around the question like a politician trying to spin things. If you are on the phone with them, listen to the tone and inflections of his/her voice.

It is rare to find someone who freely admits they are a liar, that would be a contradiction. Usually we all want to put our best foot forward and only show our good sides at the beginning of a friendship, so we try to appear to be angels. But if you pay rapt attention and do not assume anything, asking questions if you are not sure; you will be able to tell if the person you are in a friendship with shares similar values.

Do not continue being close friends with someone who tells you something today then tells you something else tomorrow about the same matter, even if it is something innocuous. Such a person is a dangerous person and cannot be trusted. Going into a relationship with a dishonest person will leave you heartbroken. It is not worth it.

What is your relationship with your parents/elders like? Do you respect them? Do you value them? Do you obey them? Do you listen to their instructions or do you consider them insignificant in your life? Does this person you have met online share your same views regarding this? How do they treat their parents?

"Children, obey your parents in the Lord for this is right. "Honour your father and mother", which is the first commandment with promise: "that it may be well with you and you may live long on earth". (Eph 6:1-3)

If you share this value towards your parents and elders, before entering into a relationship with anyone, you need to ensure he/she values their parents and elders.

Some people may not consider this important, but if you get married to a person who lacks respect for people, rest assured they will not respect you as their spouse nor have any regard for your parents.

A friend of mine met her husband online. She always wanted a man who was not a "traditional African man". Even though he was an African man, his views were not based on traditional cultural values. She appeared to be in love with everything about him, which caused her to be blinded to the fact that he had no respect for people.

Today they are married but I cannot say they are "happily married". It is a constant struggle for her. This man lacks respect for his parents, he does not care what they say or listen to them at all. His in-laws are treated the same way. Because of his pompous, arrogant attitude, most people don't want to get close to him because they don't want to be insulted or disrespected. He has a bad habit of making rash decisions which has ended up costing his family a great deal of losses because of his pride, poor attitude, inability and unwillingness to listen to wise counsel.

Even though this man is a Christian, he has not allowed the word of God to change his old ways for the same reason he refuses to seek counsel from his parents, in-laws or other elders.

This is one of the pitfalls of a long-distance relationship. Perhaps if she had taken time to observe his so-called "non-traditional" behaviours and asked questions about his value for people, she might have been able to notice this character flaw and it could have been a major red flag for her. Hence, it is important to pay attention to such behaviours and be clear to the other party regarding your values.

If you meet a person who cares less what wise and godly people say to him/her or has no regard for people, rest assured that person will have no regard for you in marriage. Don't be carried away by sweet talk, make sure that you are thinking with your head instead of your feelings before entering into a relationship.

Another value I would encourage you to have is sexual purity. In my case, I value sexual purity and Samuel did also. Hence, we were able to keep ourselves pure until marriage.

"Marriage is to be held in honour among all (that is, regarded as something of great value), and the marriage bed undefiled (by immorality or by any sexual sin); for God will judge the sexually immoral and adulterous". (Heb 13:4 AMP)

Sex is worth waiting for until marriage. There is so much to look forward to. The night we finally had sex is a night I will never forget. I always like to tell singles, God is not interested in your virginity. If you are still a virgin, this is good, please keep yourself this way until marriage. By virginity I am not just referring to ladies. Men are also to keep themselves pure until marriage. However, if you are no longer a virgin, you cannot do anything to change that. If you now have a relationship with God, make the decision that, going forward, you are going to remain celibate until marriage. However, what God is more concerned with is your sexual purity and holiness not just your virginity.

"...Be holy, for I am holy". (1Pet 1:16)

Holiness means sanctity, purity, sacredness. In this context it means being set apart for God. He demands this if, at the end of the day, we want to make Heaven (Heb. 12:14). Being sexually pure applies to every area of our lives, not just the physical act of sex. What you feed your eyes and ears with (erotic movies, pornography, etc.) will all end up in your mind, and in no time if you are not careful, you will find yourself doing those things (masturbating, anal sex, fondling with sensitive parts of your partner's body). So, it is not enough to keep your hymen intact ladies, God is asking for more. He wants you to keep every member of your body pure for His glory.

You see, when you are clear about this in your heart, you will not easily succumb to a quick moment of temptation when you are in a relationship. The first word in casualty is casual. There are many men and women who crossed the line that would honestly say they never intended to do this, they wanted to be pure until marriage. This does not happen by accident.

I am not saying it will be easy. It was quite challenging for Samuel and me whenever we were together, but because we had the same goals of keeping ourselves pure until marriage, whenever either of us hinted at straying, the other person was strong and most importantly, God's grace saw us through those heated times.

I value honesty, I value people, I value transparency, I value faithfulness. These were the values I was looking for in Samuel when we became friends, and I discovered that he possessed them; hence we were able to walk together successfully.

What are your values? Have you defined them? Are you living by God's principles? Write down your values today and constantly remind yourself of why you live by them and determine not to settle for someone who falls short in these areas.

Apart from getting your values right, it is also very important to understand God's purpose for your life. In other words, have an idea of the reason for your existence.

"Where there is no vision, the people perish…" (Prov. 29:18)

There is a reason you are still alive today. Getting married is good, but there is more to your life than just being in a relationship with somebody. There is more you can do with your life than just waiting for the right person to come your way. God created you on purpose for a purpose. There is no one else like you in the world and you need to realize that you are created as a unique individual with special abilities to make the world a better place and ultimately bring glory to God.

"Before I formed you in the womb I knew you; Before you were born I sanctified you; I ordained you a prophet to nations". (Jer. 1:5)

God is intentional about what He does. You don't just exist because He did not know what to do with His time. Like Jeremiah in the above scripture, God has set you apart for His glory to nations. You, however, need to know what this purpose is and start working towards fulfilling it.

When you are intentional about your life and live on purpose, you know where you are going; it is then easier to decide the important characteristics your future spouse must have in order to help you fulfil God's purpose for your life. For example, before I got into a relationship, I knew I was going to be involved in ministry – encouraging young women. I also intended to become a medical doctor. So, I automatically knew the person I was going to choose to marry must also be interested in ministry (not necessarily a pastor, but he must be willing to support my ministry), and be ready to support my career. I was very clear in my heart that I was not going to marry a man who only wanted me to be a stay-at-home wife! There is nothing wrong with a woman having this position, but in my case, I would not be fulfilled being at home because God had spoken to me about the usefulness of my career in the ministry He placed in my hands.

When you are clear about your journey, you are also clear about those who will not be of value to you on that journey. You will easily know who is and is not going in the same direction as yourself. You know those who will become distractions and prevent you from remaining focused in life.

I remember asking Samuel about these things during our conversations while we were just getting to know each other's family background. He mentioned that even though his mother was an accountant, she was now a housewife. I was interested in knowing why. Was this what she wanted, or it was just due to circumstances? Was that what her husband wanted her to be? Did he like his mum being a housewife? Would he desire for his future wife to be a housewife or would he want her to be a working-class wife? He told me that he preferred for his wife to work. His answers provided insights into his family and gave me an idea of what might become of my career if we got into a relationship. If he had mentioned to me that he wanted his wife to become a housewife, then I would have known that we cannot be together and I would have gone back to God in prayer.

Many people jump into a relationship without figuring out what they really want in life. Then, by the time they realize who they really are, they are married to the wrong person and end up feeling stuck and unfulfilled in their marriage. Not being able to see the person you are friends with does not mean you cannot get to know them thoroughly. Distance should not be a barrier.

My husband has gone above and beyond to support my career and ministry, and I also do all I can to support his ministry. We are committed to being used by God to bless lives around the world.

If you have not yet discovered God's purpose for your life, I would like to encourage you to do these things:

- Ask God to show you His purpose for your life.

- Find out those things you really enjoy doing and would do for people joyfully, even without getting paid for it.

- What is that thing people close to you keep telling you that you do well?

- Read books that help you to discover God's purpose for your life, such as *In Pursuit of Purpose* by Myles Munroe (This book really helped me), or *The Purpose Driven Life* by Rick Warren.

I pray that God reveals to you His purpose for your life as you earnestly seek His face. I ask this for you in Jesus' name. Amen.

It is also important that, while you are single, you love and invest in yourself. The love you have for yourself will make you to go all the way to make your life better. Don't just be satisfied with where you are, because there is a lot more you can achieve if you aim high. Register for courses that will improve you, start a business and don't be afraid to start small. You don't have to depend only on earning a monthly income. Strive to be great at whatever your hands find to do because you have the seeds of greatness inside you.

Love everything about you. Some people have never loved themselves. They keep comparing their lives to those around them, wishing their life was like that of Mr. A or Miss B. It is important for you to love everything about you. Your eyes, your legs, your complexion, your stature, your face, your breasts, your bum, your scars, your strengths, everything! Work on your areas of weakness. The Bible says you have been fearfully and wonderfully made. This means there is nothing incomplete about you and God does not do any "oh ohs". You cannot love someone the way you are supposed to when you do not love yourself. You can only give something if you already have it.

If you are someone who continuously seeks validation from people, including looking for someone to approve of your beauty, there is a strong possibility you will find yourself hooked up with the wrong person online because he/she will say all the nice things that you want to hear, sweeping you off your feet until you fall flat and get hurt. God has already validated you. You are perfect just the way you are.

In addition, do not be desperate to get into a relationship. When you just want to be in a relationship, then you will fall prey into the hands of someone who does not deserve you. A long-distance relationship is not child's play. It will stretch your emotions, your resources, and your temperament! It will also test your faith in God! If you know you have issues trusting people around you then a long-distance relationship is not for you! If for you, seeing is believing, just like Thomas in the Bible, then a long-distance relationship is not for you! Do not get into it!

"There is no fear in love; but perfect love casts out fear, because fear involves torments. But he who fears has not been made perfect in love". (1 Jn. 4:18)

Make sure that before you get into a relationship, there is a purpose to it; there is a goal in mind – marriage. Don't let anyone waste your time, money and energy chatting without having a goal in mind. If you get into a relationship without marriage as the goal, what is the point? You might as well just remain regular friends with no strings attached.

If you are getting into a long-distance relationship, realize that it is not going to be the same as other relationships where both individuals are able to spend more time with each other physically. Realize you would need to be extremely patient, especially when you don't totally understand what is going on at the other end, when it appears the other person does not understand you, or is not listening to you. The inability to see face to face can affect communication. You could type something, and it could send a wrong meaning because writing does not have tones and inflections, unlike when you say the same thing. You need to understand that this is going to be challenging, so get ready to be very tolerant.

Going into a long-distance relationship, or for that matter, any relationship requires maturity. And this type of maturity has absolutely nothing to do with age. You may be 35 years old and still not mature enough to get into a relationship. Maturity is very important in a long-distance relationship and if you are not yet mature, this kind of relationship is not for you!

Maturity in emotions – being able to control how you speak, even when you are very angry with your partner. Maturity also encompasses being able to take responsibility for your actions and not play the blame game. Maturity means you are able to apologize when you are wrong. It entails overlooking little faults and not making everything a big issue. When you are mature, you stand for what you believe and do not compromise your standards, you are not afraid to say NO to what you don't agree with! Maturity understands the difference between needs and wants and knows how to manage them appropriately. There is a difference between a preference and a conviction, and you must decide ahead of time which "hills to die on".

When you discover who you are and do not need anyone to make you feel like somebody, you know who you are, your values are well-defined, you understand that you are unique and there's no one else like you; then you are happy being YOU!

Then, as a man, it is at this point you can begin to find that person you would be able to share your life with, who compliments you and will be a suitable helpmeet in your journey of life. You could meet this person on social media and develop a friendship with her. As a lady, when you have likewise understood your worth, then you are able to choose a man who is worthy of you. A man who also knows your worth and appreciates you for who you are and will ensure that God's purpose for your life comes to pass.

Chapter 4

Developing a Friendship

A lady sent me a message requesting counsel about a guy she recently met on Facebook. She had known him for barely a month and he wanted to step up the relationship with her. He was already referring to her as "my dear". She wanted to know if this man was real or fake and she disclosed to me that she did not really know him.

I explained that you don't enter into a relationship to know who a person is. You first develop a friendship with that person to see if it can lead into a serious relationship. Take your time getting to know who you are dealing with. There is no reason to rush into being committed to someone. Go into a relationship with your very good friend, not with someone you don't really know. Get to know that person thoroughly before agreeing to a relationship with him/her. Remember, if God is in it, He will ensure it comes to pass. There is no need to rush to stop him from getting away.

In the case of the lady above, there was no way to tell if the guy was real or fake without taking the time to get to know him. Personally, I would be very uncomfortable with a guy who barely knows me referring to me as "my dear", especially without my permission. That sounds very endearing and quite alluring. I advised her to take a step back so she could see the big picture then get to know him better. I shared with her some of those things I mentioned in the previous chapter before even considering a relationship with someone.

This is a common pitfall that results in far too many people becoming broken-hearted with their online relationships. Once they think a person is interested in them, especially ladies, they just agree to a relationship without thinking it through. Do not get into a long-distance relationship with someone you have not taken the time to study properly. Don't go blindly into a relationship.

Some people blame social media for their pains in relationship and begin to say things like, "You cannot trust anyone from a distance", "you cannot believe what anyone is doing when you are not there", etc. To avoid such pains, you need to take some necessary precautions.

When you meet someone online, don't be in a hurry to meet them. Get to know who the person is first. For example, ladies, if a guy sends you a message complimenting you and wants to be your Facebook friend; before you even reply, look at his profile picture. This speaks volumes. Is he dressed like a respectable person or a tout? If he does not have a display picture, look for other pictures he has posted online or see if he has a photo album. Take time to scroll through his profile, who he is, what sort of post he shares or talks about, who his friends are, etc. This will give you a fair idea of who the person really is, what he does, likes, believes, his location, educational background, etc. You may even know if the person is a child of God or not just by checking their profile on Facebook. You will know if the account is real or a new account which is likely to be fake.

In writing this, if you are active on social media be careful of the things you share or post. For example, if you are a lady and always posting negative things about men, even if you are beautiful with an attractive profile picture, once men take a look at your posts and hateful words, that is an automatic turn off. You scare them! No man wants to date a nagging woman. Watch what you post because it is from the abundance of the heart that the mouth speaks (Matt. 12:34b) and the hand writes… No man would want to marry such a woman because not all men are bad, and no one likes a person who gripes all the time. There are many good men out there who do well, mean well and respect women, and vice versa.

Also, if you are hoping to meet someone online, it is important to have your own picture as your profile picture! I see some people who are hopeful for Mr./Miss Right use some celebrity as their profile picture or some random picture! Please use your picture! If anyone approaches you to be friends with you, there must be something about you they like. Dress nicely and take a good picture of yourself then upload it as your profile picture.

I had this nice picture of myself on hi5. Samuel told me he had seen my picture pop up a few times with a suggestion to add me as a friend, but he felt I looked like a lady who was not from his tribe. My name "Blessing" did not sound like someone from his tribe, so he did not add me as a friend. Thank God for orchestrating our meeting despite him being adamant on not adding me as a friend. Looking back now, I think that adding my tribal name "Oluwamayowa" would have cleared his doubts and maybe he would have added me as a friend. Please note that I am not against inter-tribal or inter-racial marriages, this was just Samuel's personal preference. I think that they are beautiful if both individuals are willing to learn and unlearn together. It will surprise you how your cultural background can influence the way you reason and do things. God created all humans beautifully so if you are attracted to someone from a different race for example, don't let this be a barrier if you both can walk together successfully.

It is also important to use your real name on social media platforms like Facebook. Social media is for connecting people together. A childhood friend of yours might be looking to connect with you, but because you used a wrong or fake name, they cannot find you. Spell your name properly! If your name is Damilola, for example, don't spell it Dhamilorlah! Someone who is Elizabeth will be Mhiz Liz (Miss Liz) on Facebook! Please just stop it. I see things like this all the time and I shake my head! To me this is not a serious person. That's my first impression even before I meet you. I may be wrong but that just sends a wrong message to me.

Now, after doing your research about this person decide within yourself if you would want to be their friend. I am not talking about marriage! Just being friends with the person! It could even be that you notice the two of you share the same interests, or you just like what you saw and don't mind being friends with the person.

In my own case, what attracted me to being friends with my "big brother", who connected me to Samuel was the message he sent to me after I accepted his friend request. You see, people used to send me friend requests on hi5 back then and I would just accept them without thinking. However, afterwards he sent me a private message thanking me for accepting his friend request! That message got me! No one had ever appreciated me for accepting their friend request before, so that stood out to me. I thought to myself, this is a good guy! He has good manners and he must be a gentleman. I wanted to know him better and become actual friends with such a person, so I took my time to reply and our friendship eventually produced my husband!

Get to know people very well before you begin considering them as a potential spouse. After you have understood who you are, as I mentioned in the previous chapter, the next step is to begin building friendships. There are different levels of friendship.

"Whoever believes will not act hastily". (Isa. 28: 16)

You get to know the person you have met online by asking the right questions and having good listening skills. It is important to ask questions about their backgrounds, family, career, if they are working, what sort of work they do, is he/she a believer, what values do they have, what are their areas of interest, hobbies, etc.

You do not ask all of these in a single session because that can be off-putting. You ask them gradually, and when you get an answer ask why! It is good to know more. You want to know who the person really is, if you can help the person in any way, or if the person can be of help to you in anyway. That's the essence of friendship.

For example, when Samuel and I started being friends, he knew my father was a medical doctor so he asked why I wanted to study medicine. I told him I loved to care for people and seeing them recover from their illness through my intervention. He was impressed with my answer. He later told me that he just wanted to be sure I wasn't planning to study medicine because of my dad's influence and that it was my decision. This gave him the impression that I had a vision for life, and I was walking towards achieving it.

For some people, you may just end up being casual friends and nothing more. For others, you end up becoming close friends because you both share similar values, similar ideals, similar interests, have mutual life goals and friends. These are the sort of individuals you could begin to consider as potential mates.

At this point, if you can make time to see each other, please do. Otherwise, do it whenever you both can. It is important to meet face to face and have those same conversations you had online. See if the answers are the same, watch out for their non-verbal communication. All of these are the key to ensuring you make the right choice with an online relationship. I would not advise you to enter into a relationship with someone you have not met physically, especially if you both live in the same country. It is important to find a way to see the person you are considering as a potential spouse. Well, unless your friendship is as unique as mine in every way. Realize that rather than the exception being the rule, the exception proves the rule.

In my case, Singapore was about 11,000 kilometres from Nigeria. Samuel did not have the means to come visit me in Nigeria, nor did I have the means to make our meeting a reality. We continued having daily conversations and got to know each other better. I realized we had a lot in common and I liked him.

He was born-again, a Nigerian like myself, and we were from the same state – Ekiti state in Nigeria. We both had parents who were pastors! I am intelligent and I found out he was even more intelligent than I was. He was on a Master's degree programme and planned to pursue his PhD at a very young age. He was so full of energy! He constantly challenged me to be a better person, which motivated me. He was and is a man of vision. He knew exactly where he was going in life. He knew God's purpose for his life, he told me how he saw himself 5, 10, and 20 years from then.

He was interested in ministry and I knew we were suitable for each other! I knew I would love to walk the journey of life with a man of great vision leading me! Our friendship drew me closer to God. He was so honest with me about his past relationships! I knew so much about him and he knew a lot about me. Even though we were thousands of kilometres apart, it seemed as if we were so close. I knew his friends and his parents and spoke with them a few times.

I was not surprised when he finally told me over the phone that he really liked me and wanted us to be in a serious relationship. He told me that he would like to get married to me and wanted me to be the mother of his children. This was six months into our friendship. I saw this coming and I was so excited to hear it, but I was not in a hurry to say "YES". I had to talk to God, who owns my life and knows our end from the beginning. I needed to hear God's own special thoughts to me about this young handsome, dynamic and intelligent man.

Your long-distance friendship might not be like ours where the distance was extremely long, and it would be quite expensive to frequently see each other. We did not see each other until two years after starting our relationship. I would not advise this unless your relationship is as unique as ours, one of total trust in God.

If you live in the same country, it is important to both make time to see each other as often as you can. This helps you to know and understand what he or she is like in his or her element. You see the person's house, room, you know if they are a tidy person or not. This is even better when you have surprise visits and just show up! Some people have been surprised by finding out this close friend is currently in an active relationship with another person! This should not be so, however, it will open your eyes to see things clearly and know who they really are. This is a red flag and you continue the relationship at your own peril.

At this stage, I will also counsel you not to meet your new friend in an isolated place. Do not meet in his/her house, a hotel or in any place where the two of you would be alone. When you are meeting him/her for the first time, meet in an open place such as a mall, a church service, at a function, etc.

A lady met a guy for the first time in a hotel. Her Liberian friend came to Nigeria to visit her. The day she visited him in the hotel was the same day they had sex together. Unfortunately, at the end of the day the relationship did not work out. It is not easy to trust someone you are just getting to know with your life. What if the person decides to rape you? Also, if you both are already attracted to each other, you put yourselves at the risk of falling into temptation even if you never wanted to. Hence, do not isolate yourselves when meeting for the first time or subsequent meetings.

When you begin having sex with someone you don't really know and are enjoying the sexual pleasure, you are blinded by erotic love and think you are both compatible. Erotic love cannot sustain marriage. Only the unconditional love of God (Agape) can sustain it.

When you base your friendship/relationship on Eros love you find it difficult to break away from the friendship, even when the red flags are visible, because you are so emotionally invested in it. Hence, it is always advisable to remain friends and avoid sex because at the end of it all, the relationship may not work out and no one wants to feel used and abused; you may still continue to be good friends.

A lady based in Nigeria sent me a message regarding a guy she had been in a relationship with for two years. This guy, although Nigerian, was based in Italy. They were childhood friends but only reconnected after many years when he got to Italy. To make a long story short, she does not know what kind of work he is doing because he told her she would not understand. She does not know any of his friends over there, and he told her the reason he has been unable to visit her is his paperwork is not yet complete for his visa.

At this point I sensed that he was an illegal immigrant in Italy, which she admitted he was. She then went on to tell me that when she tried calling him recently a woman picked up and she heard a baby's voice in the background. When she confronted him they got into a quarrel. He finally claimed the lady was his landlady, which I found hard to believe! So, for the past two years, she was seeing this man in an online relationship but had no idea he was living with a lady? She explained he does not tell her a lot about himself but reassured her that when they get married he will explain everything.

I could not believe she was continuing this relationship with a person who is secretive and has a dishonest lifestyle. What exactly have they been talking about for the past two years? This is definitely a red flag. In my opinion, this guy is probably married to an Italian citizen with the hope of using this marriage to become a citizen after a few years of marriage. Then he will suddenly and rudely divorce her once she has fulfilled her usefulness to him, freeing him up to marry this lady in Nigeria.

Why in the world would you settle for such a cad who already has his life complicated with shady and dishonest stuff? Are you so desperate to be in a relationship or get married that you think this is the best you can get, and you will not find a better man? These were my questions to the lady. Unless she wants a complicated life that will probably end up in disaster, then it is up to her. In the future, if she continued with this man, she will not be able to blame anyone but herself for the consequences of her decision. Some ladies fall into this trap with an online lover. Please do not fall prey to their wily ways! If you are friends with a person who is dodgy, don't get close to such a person, let alone enter into a relationship with him/her. Don't be so gullible.

Many people have been scammed through online dating. Don't be one of them. If you are not desperate and know your worth, it will help you to avoid falling into such a trap. In addition to this, if your online friend/partner is always demanding for money from you while sharing very pitiable stories or telling you about one business deal or the other, watch out! This person may just be out to deceive you for his/her own selfish gains and is not genuine. Be very careful and do your due diligence before giving your money out to such a person.

I will end this chapter by saying that you should make sure God is leading you to the person before beginning a long-distance relationship. Some people would say you don't have to hear from God before you get married. I would counsel that it is good to hear from God because when you do, then you've got a word to hold on to when trials and tribulations come, which they surely will.

When things look as though you missed it and the storms come through, you can confidently go back to God to see you through. You can rest assured that your relationship/marriage boat will not capsize! This is key. You can never go wrong when God is involved.

God can speak to you in various ways – through His Word, through dreams, through His ministers, through a still small voice to you, and others. No matter which way you have heard Him speak to you, if what you heard contradicts His Word, then know that it is not God speaking to you! In other words, put His Word side by side with whatever you have seen, read or heard. His Word is the most authentic. Don't wait until you are ready to choose a life partner before you begin to seek the voice of God. If you wait till that time, you are likely to be confused as you will hear many voices speaking to you and would wonder which is God's. If you are keen to hear from God, begin to develop a relationship with Him now by studying the Bible regularly and praying to Him. This way, you are tuned to hearing from Him easily when He speaks. Don't get discouraged if you start doing this and it appears you are not hearing anything, just continue, very soon, you will hear Him speak to you even through your day and you will know He is the one talking.

A relationship with God can be likened to getting to know a new person. You do not know all about the person in a day. It would take some time to understand when the person is joking and when the person isn't. It will take some time to know the person's voice even when you cannot see the person. This is similar with a relationship with God. Invest time into your relationship with now. Having God guide you is a huge asset.

In my own case, after my Samuel told me how he wanted us to be in a relationship – courtship and that he desired to marry me in the future, although I remember hearing God that very first night, I still wanted Him to speak to me to be sure I was doing the right thing. I honestly thought that night was a joke and wanted God to be serious with me.

This was going to be my first relationship and I really desired for it to be my only one. I did not want to be heartbroken, I did not want to miss it, I did not want to make a fool of myself by going into a relationship with a man I had not met. I never heard of a long-distance relationship like that before; it sounded crazy, but I was not afraid to go into it if I was certain God was in it.

I decided to take time to fast and pray for a few days. I kept on talking to Samuel during this time and told

Him that I was waiting to hear God confirm His word to me regarding our relationship. Prior to this, Samuel had prayed about us and told me he was confident God was leading him to me.

He told his parents and they were confident that God was in it. He told one of his fathers in the Lord about us and he received a vision about both of us, which was another confirmation. God had also spoken to my parents about us. However, I still needed my own word! Don't enter into a relationship based solely on the words people have received on your behalf. If God can speak to them about you, God can speak to you too because He wants you to know His mind. You just need to have a relationship with Him and be ready to listen when He does. Go into the relationship with your own conviction.

Dear reader, God is faithful. On the 14th of March 2008, I received a word from God regarding Samuel and me. I also received a vision from God regarding His assignment for us as a couple. Eleven years after, we are fulfilling the vision that God gave me. All glory to Him. I was so happy to receive my own word.

Words cannot describe the excitement Samuel had when I told him it was a "YES" over the phone. He was over the moon, in fact he flung his phone out of joy! It was as if he had won a million dollars!

We prayed together on that day and made sure to place our relationship in God's hands. We asked God to guide us on our journey to the unknown. In tears, even though we had no idea when we were going to finally see each other, we trusted the One who owns the future to make it happen as quickly as possible and to make a way. The peace we had about our relationship was reassuring.

Samuel had relocated to New Zealand and was determined to see me somehow. One day, he found out that his doctorate research would be totally paid for, so he decided to choose a topic for his thesis and use Nigeria as a case study. Doing this meant that his expenses would include travelling to Nigeria to interview people, which would be paid for, and at the same time, he would have the opportunity to meet me! This was some of the best news ever! I would finally be able to see the man I've been in a relationship with for so long.

"Behold…I will even make a road in the wilderness, and rivers in the desert". (Isa. 43:19b)

"The counsel of the LORD stands forever". (Ps. 33:11)

We both started looking forward to his coming and I was super excited that I was finally going to meet the love of my life. Yes, he was the love of my life already because I knew there was no going back on him no matter what! He spent three months in Nigeria for his research. Even though he was busy interviewing people for his data collection and I was busy with lectures in medical school; we both arranged to meet each other as often as we could. We went for lunch dates, dinner dates, spent time going to church together, spent time studying God's word and praying together, spent time talking together, meeting with friends and family together and asking more and more questions. He lived with a close family of his and I often visited him there while he came to my university.

On the 23rd of July, a day I will never forget. Samuel and I set eyes on each other for the first time at the airport. I was accompanied by my mum and younger sister to pick him up. We waited for about two hours, standing at the Muritala Mohammed International Airport in Lagos, Nigeria but when he finally came out, we both could not contain our joy.

I ran to meet him and hug him. He was so excited, he lifted me off my feet and carried me with so much energy. I knew he was the one for me, I was at peace. Even though he was limping after sustaining a knee injury from playing soccer a few days before his flight and had a bandage around his knee, to me he was the most handsome man in the entire universe. I should also mention that Samuel has mild bow legs. I knew this from pictures he sent to me and it was evident when I saw him, but I loved him just the way he was. His content (character) was more of a priority to me than his physical appearance and I loved what I saw.

I observed his behaviour, to ascertain who and what he claimed he was. I observed his dress sense, his style, his body language when we don't agree on an issue, his attitude to my parents and siblings, his relationship with God, his respect to time... everything and I was convinced I was on the right track.

On the 18th of September 2010, he went down on one knee during one of my visits and formally proposed to me. I can't even remember all the beautiful things he said to me before asking me to marry him. I was just in awe and I said "YES" of course! He slipped on an engagement ring he bought in New Zealand on my finger. I honestly had no idea he had made such plans and I was not expecting it at all. I was pleasantly surprised and was grateful to him.

We knew that our relationship was peculiar, and we wouldn't have the luxury of seeing each other frequently, so our parents decided to have a mini-formal family introduction. An introduction ceremony is a tradition in the part of Nigeria where I come from for those who are planning to get married. It is an opportunity for both families of the intending bride and groom to meet formally and agree to the relationship/marriage of their children.

Although my mother-in-love (I don't call Samuel's parents in-laws. I see them as my parents too) could not make it as she was in Malaysia with my sisters-in-law; she was with us over the phone and formally gave her consent to my relationship with Samuel and prayed for us. My father-in-love was present with a few other family and friends. We celebrated in a little way and both families were confident it was the beginning of great things in the lives of their children and in their families.

If you are in a long-distance friendship and scared of taking it to the next level because you are not sure what the future holds, I understand how you feel but I will counsel you to take your fears to the One who owns the future. He knows what your future is like and He will guide you and make your life and relationship beautiful. Don't be afraid to take that step. If God is in it, He will see you through just like He saw us through. It's been 11 years knowing him and I can confidently tell you that I have no regrets I went into that long-distance relationship.

Chapter 5

BE ACCOUNTABLE

Being accountable means being answerable to someone for something – in this case your relationship. As soon as you are sure that you are willing to get into a relationship with your friend and he or she becomes your partner, do not keep it a secret!

In my particular case, my parents were aware of our friendship and I kept them informed at every stage. The day Samuel shared with me his intentions to marry me, I told them and they prayed along with me. By the time I was convinced God was leading us to walk the path of a long-distance relationship, I carried them along with us during each step.

In the very beginning, I must let you know that it was not easy to have my parents agree with my close friendship with Samuel, especially my dad. My parents are pastors and are very old school. They wanted the best for me and did not want me to get hurt, which I totally understood. This new technology and way of doing things was foreign to them. My dear dad could not see how a long-distance relationship could work; in fact, he was close to telling me to stop chatting with Samuel and wasting my time.

My mum and I on the other hand were very close. She was my best friend and I showed her almost all the chats I had with Samuel. In fact, she told me a few times before he finally opened up to me that she sensed he was wanting more than just a friendship and I would just laugh about it.

You see, I had never been in a relationship before, so I needed guidance and my mum was there for me.

It is important to always seek guidance from those who know better. Before embarking on a long-distance relationship and while you are in it, speak to your parents, speak to your mentors, speak to your pastor/spiritual leader, speak to those you trust, relationship counsellors, and be willing to honestly meditate on their advice. Be accountable! Do not go into a relationship with someone who refuses to be accountable to anybody! Such a person is dangerous to be with!

My mum did not express any worries or fears about my long-distance friend before we got into a relationship, even though Dad was not too keen on it. He did not think it made any sense to be in a relationship with a person you had never seen and have no idea when you will ever see each other. I tried to make him understand that this man in question was God's will for me and prayed and trusted that God would speak to him.

One day while he was in the bathroom, God spoke to him, saying that he (my father) had been praying to Him to grant me a man after His heart. Now this prayer has been answered but he is kicking against it! Then God asked him, "Do you want her to marry an unbeliever?" At that point, my father gave up the fight and prayed for our friendship. Although it still didn't make sense to him, He told me that I had his support and he was willing to let God have His way in our lives. Hearing this brought so much joy and happiness to my heart.

If you decide to embark on a long-distance relationship according to God's leading and meet with disagreements from your parents, don't argue, don't fight them, instead listen to them, speak to them, and ask God to open their eyes while also being willing to have your eyes opened, perhaps they see something critical that you don't. Don't stop praying, don't stop believing. Don't be rude to them, and don't get married without their blessings. It is very important that you listen to whatever their concerns are and see how you can reach a compromise with them. Many parents want the best for their children and their disagreements with your relationship are almost always born out of love.

If you are in a long-distance relationship with someone and you have not seen or spoken to his friends or family members, then I would be very worried about such a relationship. How can you be investing your time, energy, emotions, resources, and all that you have in a relationship with someone and have no idea who his/her family members are? This is why some long-distance relationships fail.

When you are courting someone you cannot see, it is important to know the person's friends and befriend them also. These are the people who can help you keep your partner in check and disclose anything dodgy that your partner may be doing that they know you would not support.

In my own case, my big brother was helpful in keeping Samuel in check, especially at the beginning of our relationship as there was a lady in his church at that time who really liked him. Also, I was in touch with his parents. Even though we had not met physically at the beginning of our relationship, we were occasionally calling one another over the phone. They were already referring to me as their daughter. They are such wonderful parents! They would even buy me gifts and send them to Nigeria! They would call me on my birthday to pray for me and lots more. I could not wait to officially have them as parents! I remember one day, my mother-in-love told me before I came along she had been praying for God to give her a daughter, not a daughter-in-law. She wanted a loving and God-fearing lady for her son, and she was confident she had found this person.

"The desire of the righteous will be granted". (Prov. 13: 24b)

You see, when family members are aware of such relationships, it makes you both more committed. Even if one person is tempted to do something silly, the good people around him or her and knowledge of family members, pastors etc. will always caution such a person with the fear of God. I remember my Father-in-love cautioning Samuel a few times, saying, "Make that relationship work". He would always check up on him to ask how our relationship was going.

There was a time Samuel and I had a major misunderstanding. Looking back, I honestly cannot remember what caused it. All I remember is we both decided to call it quits that day over the phone. We were both very angry with each other. Anyway, when Samuel informed his parents about the end of our relationship can you guess what they told him? They told him to go back and apologize and make sure we got back together, which he did. Now, imagine if he had no one to be accountable to? That would possibly have been the end of our relationship and this book you are reading would never have been written.

If you are able to meet your partner's parents, mentors, friends, and other important family members physically, please do. This way they can put a face to the name they keep hearing about. You are able to see and interact with them better and they are also able to know who you are. Also, it gives you a clearer picture of your partner's background and provides an opportunity to ask your own questions and obtain first-hand information.

My relationship was very unique. I first met one of Samuel's spiritual parents in Nigeria. He told this man about me so I went to worship in his church on one of the Sundays in year 2008. We had conversations together and he prayed with me. Later, in 2009, I met Samuel's dad when he came to Nigeria to visit my parents to get to know them and declare his son's intention for me to be his wife in the near future. It was an unofficial introduction, but it was beautiful. They both connected and I was very happy.

You see, being accountable is very important because there are times when both of you will face challenges in your relationship or even in marriage which you might not be able to settle without the intervention of more mature people both of you honour and respect and are willing to listen to. They would then be able to pray for you and constantly check up on the two of you.

There was the story of a lady in a relationship with a man who was not accountable to anyone. This guy just lived his life alone, had no one he looked up to, had no one who cautioned him or held him to account. By the time she married him, and they started struggling in their marriage she felt he did not value her or care about her feelings. She had no one to report him to! He did not respect her pastor, he had no father, he had nobody! This wife found herself in a very difficult situation and had to keep praying for him. So, please, do not marry anyone who has no regard for authority! Do not go into a relationship with anyone who has no one he/she listens to. It is going to be catastrophic!

CHAPTER 6

COMMUNICATE REGULARLY

A long-distance relationship cannot survive without regular communication! All relationships are sustained through communication, and in a relationship where you do not physically interact this is even more pertinent. Without communication there is no information, and without information there is no understanding, and without understanding conflicts are inevitable. Consistent communication is pivotal to the success of any long-distance relationship. Communication must come from a pure and sincere heart; there must not be any hypocrisy or deception. Furthermore, let your words be true; this is the Bible way of communicating:

"But let your 'Yes' be 'Yes,' and your 'No' 'No.' For whatever is more than these is from the evil one". (Matt. 5:37)

"Therefore, putting away lying, 'Let each one of you speak truth with his neighbour, 'for we are members of one another". (Eph. 4:25)

"Let your speech always be with grace, seasoned with salt, that you may know how you ought to answer each one". (Col. 4:6)

"Let love be without hypocrisy. Abhor what is evil. Cling to what is good". (Rom. 12:9)

It is challenging enough not being able to see each other physically, so communicating is the only means of interaction you have to know the person thoroughly before entering into a journey of no return called marriage.

You see, courtship is a period of interviewing; you need to continue asking relevant questions and not assume or expect that the person is who you think they should be. Assumptions can be dangerous. For instance, don't expect the person to just know you are tired because you just got home from a busy day at work. You need to let him/her know you are tired and prefer to talk later because you want to take a nap rather than get grumpy or angry with them for having a conversation with you when you are exhausted and on edge. Be open to saying things the way they are without sugar-coating them or giving a false impression.

Samuel and I ensured that we communicated every single day, even if it was for just a few minutes! There was hardly ever a day that went by that we did not communicate. The time difference was a huge challenge. Sometimes it was 11 hours and other times of the year we were 12 hours apart due to daylight saving! In other words, when my day in Nigeria was just starting, he was preparing to go to bed and vice versa, but we made it work.

While I was in medical school, he was doing his PhD and working in the mornings. Here is an example of one of our typical days:

When he wakes up about 6 am which is 6 pm Nigerian time (usually I am the one who called to wake him up because it would be evening on my end and I was usually free. He was happy to let my call be his alarm clock and we did this for years), we would talk briefly for a few minutes. I would ask how his night went and if he slept well and he would also ask about my day. Usually this conversation would last for 5-10 minutes and then I let him get ready for work. Then he might call me on his way to work or we would chat back and forth while he was on the train, which was usually about an hour ride. We used BlackBerry messenger then and it was very helpful. Once he arrived at work, I knew he was unable to make phone calls or chat with me so I continued my evening while he started his day at work.

I sometimes sent him a beautiful email to express my love for him so he could read it during his break. I should also mention that Samuel liked to wake up to messages or pictures from me. So, I made it a point to take pictures of myself on most days and sent it to him. This made him very happy and sometimes made his day. Whenever I defaulted, he was not happy with me and I had to make it up to him. He regularly sent me emails and text messages. Honestly, I couldn't catch up with his messages. He was and still is very romantic.

He usually called me during his short 15 minute break, sometime between 10:30 and 11:00 pm Nigerian time. We would chat and then bid me good night. Some nights when I slept very late, we could talk some more after his work around 12 noon NZ time (he worked for 4 hours daily).

When I woke up in the morning, I gave him a call or he sometimes woke me up when he wasn't busy. During my day, whenever I was free, I quickly called him, or we chatted. He often told me how his day went, and we talked about different things including random jokes. If I was busy, he called or texted me before he went to sleep at night. This was our routine until we got married.

Even though we were thousands of kilometres away from each other, we remained close. I could tell you where Samuel was each time and what he was doing, and he could do the same with me. A few times when his parents were unable to reach him, they called me to ask if I heard from him and knew what he might be up to, and I was usually a great help! This is how your long-distance relationship should be. Distance was not a barrier to our relationship at all.

You may not be able to have a routine like ours depending on both of your schedules and circumstances, but it is important not to allow a day to go by without communicating with each other in some capacity. I would even suggest praying in the morning together. Although we had our day of praying and fasting, we didn't think about starting our day together with prayers when we called each other over the phone.

If you are in a relationship and your partner is against communicating with you regularly, always giving excuses why he/she cannot talk or chat, then you should be worried. It shows, to a large extent, that you are not their priority. Human beings always make time for whatever is important to them. So, if he/she is not willing to make sacrifices to ensure both of you keep the line of communication going, I'm afraid your relationship may not work. Anyone who cannot make you a priority now will not make you a priority after you are married.

Communicating in a long-distance relationship requires paying rapt attention to the other person, as many times you cannot see the person's body language (unless during video calls). Because you are missing this important sense you have to listen beyond the words (a good listening skill is very essential) and pick up on the emotions of the person. You need to know when they are serious and when they are joking, even though he or she is saying the same words. There is a difference between hearing and listening. Make sure you are not only hearing but listening to your partner.

Technology has made communication so much easier than it used to be where letters could take months to get to someone. Now, with the development of all sorts of platforms like WhatsApp, Viber, Facebook, Instagram, Telegram and so many others, just to mention a few, you can talk to someone halfway around the world instantaneously. You can also do live video calls for free, so long as you have some data on your phone. Bear in mind that regular communication is not so cheap, it will come at a cost but it is worth it if you both must succeed in the relationship. There is no reason not to communicate. Emailing is also a great tool.

If you want to make your long-distance relationship a success, you need to keep asking questions. There is no stupid question. Don't be afraid to ask questions and let your partner know your likes and dislikes, even from a distance. Realize that you are planning to commit your life to this person, and you need to know if it is going to be worth your while. If you have a partner who shuts you up when you ask him/her personal questions or hides things from you, please don't become involved with such a person. Marrying that kind of person is dangerous. Don't stop communicating. Realize that the two of you are not in a business relationship but have become best friends in courtship, with marriage as the goal.

Talk about where you both would like to settle down; which of you needs to move? I knew I would have to move before entering into a relationship with Samuel because he hinted that he would not be coming back to live in Nigeria. If you have to move like I did, would you be happy to do so? Do you see your future in the country or state your partner is in? Do you see things working out for you? This might be one of the scary things about long-distance relationships. For me, I had to think about leaving my comfort zone and my parents to travel to an unknown land. This is something you both must talk about and come to a conclusion on during your courtship. If neither of you is willing to move, there is no point in continuing to waste your time in that relationship.

However, if you are scared of relocating like I was, then just trust God. I was worried about several exams I would have to write after becoming a medical doctor in Nigeria before being able to practise medicine in New Zealand. To worsen my fear and uncertainty, I heard things were not looking good regarding jobs in New Zealand as an international medical graduate.

I checked with Samuel a few times to see if he was going to change his mind and settle in Nigeria, but he remained adamant he was not. Even my dad encouraged him to spend at least one year to do his National Youth Service Corps (NYSC), which is a compulsory service for all Nigerian citizens after graduating from the university. However, since he did not see himself ever having to do anything again in

Nigeria and was very certain that He was led by God to move to New Zealand for a purpose bigger than just his doctorate degree, he felt spending even one year in Nigeria would be a waste. I had to depend on God completely. I trusted God would make a way for my career when the time came since He was the one leading me in this way. I had no idea what to expect, but I trusted God that New Zealand would favour both of us and perfect all that concerned our career.

Even though he was not interested in leaving New Zealand, I was very confident that he fully supported my career and had promised to do all he could to ensure I was fulfilled in my chosen career. To the glory of God, today, I am practising medicine in New Zealand. It was a very tough journey, but with God's help and my husband's unwavering support, we eventually got there. We are both citizens of the country including our children. In addition, God has settled us in this country and we have been able to buy our own house too! These and more are our testimonies. God is faithful if only you completely depend on Him.

My favourite passage of the Bible says ***"Trust in the Lord with all your heart and lean not on your own understanding; In all your ways acknowledge Him,***

and He shall direct your paths". (Prov. 3:5-6). Realize that the passage talks about trusting God with all your heart and not some of your heart. He is a reliable God and if He promises a thing, He will fulfil it. There is no disappointment with Him. He makes all things beautiful in His own perfect time.

Another important conversation we had before we got married was regarding sex. Some people don't think that it is important to talk about this but sexual incompatibility has led to many marriages coming to an end sadly. No matter how spiritual you are, as long as you are human, you have sexual hormones present in your body. In addition, there are expectations and perceptions that you have about sex in marriage. Hence, it is necessary that you find out the other person's ideology about sex and see if you both can walk together successfully. Some people have been sexually active in the past, so they are likely to be experienced with different sexual styles, have knowledge of their favourite style and have a good idea of the frequency to which they would need sex in marriage.

In our case, Samuel was the experienced one, so he was able to share with me his preferences and even though I was a virgin, he wanted to know if I was going to be willing to learn, if I was going to be able to meet his needs sexually, what my perception about sex was Of course, I was willing to learn at the right time which is in marriage and I have really learnt a lot!

It would interest you to know that some people think that sex is just for child bearing and so they only have sex when they are planning to have children. If for instance, you are the sort of person that would desire to have sex at least once a day and you marry such a person, you are likely to be frustrated in that marriage and this can lead to infidelity. Hence, I would advise you to talk about it. Samuel and I had this conversation away from each other, so the chances of falling into temptation were slim.

Do not leave any stone unturned, don't be shy about asking these questions with your partner – what are the sexual things you consider unholy in marriage? What's their view about oral sex in marriage for instance? Talk about it! Has your partner been sexually abused before? This is a traumatic experience for anyone and if he or she is yet to heal, it could affect your marriage, talk about it and see how you can be of help.

Another important conversation to have is how many kids do you both want to have. Some people want many kids, others want a few, while some do not want any children! It is important to ask. Samuel and I wanted four (two boys and two girls), but by the time we had two boys we decided to hang up our boots and retire in this department. Ha ha ha. Don't just assume that your partner wants children, talk about it.

It is also pertinent to discuss what happens if God chooses for you not to have children. Realize that children are a gift from God. The purpose of marriage is not only to have children. Some people may not have children; it doesn't mean that the marriage should come to an end. Samuel and I were keen to adopting children if we couldn't bear children of our own. This was our agreement. You see, adoption is not sinful. I have heard of couples who adopted children and then God opened their wombs. What does your partner think of adoption or fertility methods? Would he/she be keen towards it or are they against them? Know this before you say, "I do".

Also talk about contraception. Does your partner believe in contraception or does he/she think it is sinful? What sort of contraception would you both be willing to use? Talk about these things and come to an agreement before you get married. Contraception helps you have only the number of children you can successfully look after. You both need to reach an agreement regarding this. Samuel and I agreed on no hormonal contraception until we had the number of children we desired. We agreed to use condoms after marriage during my ovulation period. I had a very regular menstrual cycle which we decided would work for us.

Talk about your finances. Joint or separate accounts? Who will be in charge of the finances? How much debt/savings does each of you have? Who is the spender or saver between you both? Who would be your next of kin in marriage? Some people choose their sibling or parent as their next of kin instead of their spouse. Talk about it so you are not surprised after marriage.

Samuel and I initially decided we were going to have a joint account in marriage, but a few years into our marriage, we realized this was not working for us, so we decided to have separate personal accounts in addition to our joint account; and this has been working for us. Talk about these things.

The influence of a third party in your home. Will friends/family members be living with you? Would you be discussing your family business with parents? Talk about it. I would advise you not to allow anyone to live with you during the first two years of marriage if you have had a long-distance relationship. You need time to blend together and allowing a third party into the equation may not help the two of you to work on the differences you may begin to notice while living together.

The church you both will start going to once you get married (this is if you both attend different denominations). I would suggest that both of you to attend the same church once you get married to foster unity in the home, especially when you begin to have children.

Talk about your love languages. The book, *The Five Love Languages* by Dr. Garry Chapman would be of help to you both. Know each other's love language and speak them fluently. Courtship is the best time to begin practising these love languages so by the time you are married, you are fluently speaking each other's language without any struggle. Knowing your partner's love language helps you to constantly put smiles on their face and keeps him/her thinking of you.

I would counsel you to communicate your likes and dislikes. I didn't like Samuel putting his hands around another lady's waist while taking pictures. I saw a few of his pictures with ladies and told him I didn't like it. I was ok with him putting his hand on their shoulder but nowhere else.

He initially could not understand why I had a problem with it and said that it was nothing, but he stopped doing it because he respected my views. This was a rule we had in our relationship. We were committed to honouring comments about each other's dislikes and making efforts to change. There was another picture he took where he carried a lady he called his "sister". I did not hide my feelings at all about this too. I did not like it and told him not to do that again, which he stopped also.

You see, Samuel is a people person and is very friendly. He does all those things with no strings attached but I just don't feel comfortable with them. He respected my disapproval. Some people would see these things and get angry with the other person without initially expressing their disapproval. Speak out regarding what you don't like. If you do not speak out, the other person will continue with the habit and things might not change in marriage.

If you would not like your fiancée to hug another guy, let her know. You both should be open and sincere with each other. As an individual, you have your personal preferences, so don't keep mute in a relationship and then begin to nag in marriage.

It is important that you both have boundaries in your relationship and talk about the limits your fiancé(e) can go regarding relationships with the opposite sex. Some people would not approve of a hug from the opposite sex. I did not mind this.

Talk about how to resolve conflict when you both are at loggerheads. Which of you is the more temperamental? One person needs to be calm while the other person is boiling. It is always important to be patient with each other. Talk about your language of apology. The book *The Five Languages of Apology* by Garry Chapman and Jennifer Thomas will help throw more light on this. Both of you can read this book together. Samuel does not believe that I'm really sorry, even when I say "I'm sorry". I need to go all the way to admit that I have done wrong and that I regret my actions and mention the things I plan to do to prevent such mistakes from happening again. Only then does he accept my apology! I found this apology type extremely difficult. I mean, he only needs to tell me "I'm sorry" and I will sincerely accept his apology, so why can't he just accept my sorry too? We used to quarrel a lot about this until I had to accept that this was his own language of apology. Know your partner's apology language and speak it to help avoid unnecessary arguments and prevent malice, so you can keep the line of communication going.

If you both can't seem to agree on anything and find you are always at loggerheads, then you might not be compatible with each other. Seek counsel from your trusted mentor, spiritual leader or parents.

Talk about building a future together. You see, when some people find the right person, all that is on their mind is the wedding date and they begin to plan for the wedding. This should not be so! If you begin to plan just for the wedding and you haven't done your due diligence to get to know the person on a deeper level, which comes with time, you might have yourself to blame.

CHAPTER 7

TRUST EACH OTHER

I mentioned at the beginning of this book that if you have problems trusting people you can see, then don't bother venturing into a relationship with someone you cannot see because you will only end up frustrating yourself and the other person.

Honesty and transparency are the backbone of any long-distance relationship. If you build your relationship on lies, rest assured the relationship will collapse; it is just a matter of time. It is important to be completely transparent with each other and this starts while you are both friends. You must have realized that you both value honesty, hence the reason you are able to walk together.

While being friends with Samuel, I initially observed that he was a very honest person and extremely down to earth. He opened up to me about his past relationships, his escapades, his weaknesses, everything, without me even asking much about these things. You see, the very first day he spoke to me over the phone (my big brother had passed the phone over to him), he told me that I should just be myself and we'll see where our friendship will lead. That got me too.

Throughout our relationship, our policy was honesty. We told each other, even if it is going to hurt the other person, we would still both say the truth! We always did.

Don't ever hide anything from your significant other. It is not good; it is not fair. Let the person know some important details about your past. For example, if you have been married before, if you have child(ren), if you were in previous relationships and what led to the break-up. All of these help you know the person better and being able to disclose all this to him/her is very vital. Don't let the person find out after you are married. This breaks the bond of trust!

Realize that what you sow into your relationship you will reap. Where you sow transparency and similar virtues, you will always reap love in abundance! Sowing falsehood is like sowing thorns and thistles, it is only a matter of time before the yield will nearly choke the life out of the two partners and anyone around them.

"They that sow the wind, shall reap whirlwind". (Hos. 8:7)

If you want to be trusted by your partner, you need to prove yourself to be trustworthy. Say only what you mean and mean what you say. Be a person of integrity.

One other reason why we found it easy to trust each other was because we were open to each other about our relationships with the opposite sex. I didn't have many male friends while he had quite a few female friends, but he always told me about them. For some of them, whose friendship I was worried about, I suggested ways for him to be careful. Also, because I knew his daily routine, it was easy for me to trust him. The same is true with him regarding me.

We trusted each other with our passwords. Email, social media passwords, and so on. There was nothing to hide. Our genuine love for each other made it easy to trust each other. We still do, even now.

For those who started out being in close proximity with each other and then, for one reason or the other (career, job, etc), one person had to leave the city or even the country for a long time, it is important for you to both keep being transparent and open with each other.

The reality of life is, you will eventually meet someone who appears to be smarter, richer, more intelligent, more attractive and more spiritual than the person you have chosen. Even when you get married, you will still meet these kinds of people. It is your commitment to your spouse that keeps you going, ensure that you don't lose focus off what drew your attention to your partner.

Be careful of your close relationships with the opposite sex when you are committed to someone already. Sometimes if you realize your interactions with such people is putting your relationship in danger, you might need to watch out or limit your communication with those friends. This may sound harsh but you have to decide what is more of a priority to you – losing your partner or losing the other friend.

If your partner is concerned about your friendship, then it is advisable to listen to them and not ignore what he/she is saying. Ignoring your partner's concerns shows you do not have any regard for him/her, and if your partner does not listen to your fears or worries about a relationship he is having with someone else, be sure that he/she will not listen to you in marriage. This is a red flag.

Samuel had this other lady he met on Facebook a few years after we started our relationship and they got to talking. He became very good friends with her. She was also in Nigeria and he had not met her before. He told me a lot about her and told her a lot about me. In fact, I spoke to her over the phone a few times and she was aware of our relationship. However, I became uncomfortable when I noticed them becoming close and their conversations had gotten very personal. He would also communicate with her almost every day also and our conversations were about their conversations! I sensed they both were beginning to develop feelings for each other and I later found out that I was right. I had to tell him to choose between the two of us. I was not going to beg him or speak to her. I made it clear that he had to either stop talking to her or stop talking to me. He had to sever his relationship with her so we could go forward. This was only possible because we were open with each other and respected each other.

You may not see each other but believe the best of each other, pray for each other and listen to each other. Don't let anyone or anything come between the two of you. I pray for God to help you.

In conclusion, always remember the Word of God that admonishes true Christians in the way of relating together.

"Let all bitterness, wrath, anger, clamour, and evil speaking be put away from you, with all malice. And be kind one to another, tender-hearted, forgiving one another, even as God in Christ forgave you". (Eph. 4:31-32)

Chapter 8

Do Things Together

Although you are miles apart, a long-distance relationship can be so much fun. There are a number of fun activities you can both can engage in while far away from each other to strengthen the bond between you. One of the ways Samuel and I made our long-distance relationship a success was through sharing God's word together regularly, praying regularly and fasting together.

Are you wondering how this can happen in a long-distance relationship? It is very possible and simple! You see, the Bible says that a three-fold cord is not easily broken. At the beginning of our relationship, we encouraged each other to study the Bible and discuss over the phone what we both learnt from the passages we read. Samuel motivated me in this area. I must confess I was not used to studying the Bible daily. Our relationship drew us both closer to God. Your relationship should draw you both closer to God and not away from him. If you are in a relationship where you find yourself drawing farther and farther away from God, you are in the wrong relationship! Examine yourself.

Even if you don't know what to talk about that day, sharing the Bible verse and talking about what you learnt opens up conversations about other topics and hearing your partner's view about things you didn't even consider talking about. It helps you see how they reason, and know their depth and understanding of God's word. I remember that I just discussed the moral lessons of what I read from the Bible; Samuel on the other hand would give me revelations from his own study! This wowed me a lot, I was confident he was the right person to lead and draw me closer to God.

We fasted every Wednesday, after which we would both pray to break our fast at different times due to the time difference. We would pray for our relationship, pray for our future, pray for the marriage ahead of us, pray for our unborn children, our parents, our careers, our ministries, we would pray for everything! We did this for years and we are still fasting and praying together, by God's grace.

There's the popular saying, "a couple that prays together stays together". This was one of our secrets! If you are courting someone in a long-distance relationship, you can fast and pray together. This strengthens the spiritual bond in your relationship and keeps the enemy away. It helps you both grow together spiritually. Share the Scriptures together, edify each other, encourage each other, prophesy into each other's lives. This is the foundation of a Kingdom marriage.

We were not boring lovers, we played together also! I must confess Samuel was the one who usually initiated the games we played online. We played truth or dare. This was one way of asking questions you may consider awkward to ask. For example, I remember using such opportunities to ask if he had any close female friends, I wanted to know if I needed to be worried/warn him to be careful.

We also googled several games for partners which we downloaded and played to have fun with each other. The winner would dare the other person to do something unusual, which was really fun for both of us.

We used to read books together, especially relationship books and discuss them over the phone where we shared our thoughts and asked questions about what each of us thought. One of the books we read together was, *The Five Love Languages of Singles*. The book opened my eyes to my husband's love language which was physical touch at that time. Even though I was not physically present with him, he made me to understand what it means to him when he is touched by someone he adores and cherishes. He explained to me how he would like me to touch him. Oh! Samuel loves public display of affection and he told me to expect all of that whenever he comes to visit.

I was not used to public display of affection, but because this was what love meant to him, I started learning to hug people, to hold hands, to pat people on the back… because even beyond our relationship, I realized also that this was what love meant to some other people. The book opened my eyes to a lot of things! I did my best to speak this love language to him whenever we were together. I would hold his hands while we went for walk, I hugged him so many times.

At this point, I would like to talk about setting boundaries in your relationship. When distance is a barrier and all you do is talk, the moment you are physically in touch there is the tendency to go all out to explore each other's bodies. There is a tendency to want to kiss, caress, and if you are not careful and don't handle your emotions well, both of you may have sex! Yes! This is the truth. Remember, you are in love with someone who you are physically and emotionally attracted to. Your sex hormones could peak in the heat of the moment, hence the reason both of you need to agree on boundaries that you will not cross.

Samuel and I agreed that we were going to remain pure in our relationship. Our boundaries included meeting outside - cafes, restaurants, malls, etc. If I was meeting him in his house (since he was living with a family), his door would always be open; the same thing applied if he came to my dorm room in the university.

However, sometimes we just wanted "our privacy" and honestly this landed us into a big mess! One day, we were watching a movie together on his laptop in his house. That day we had prayed, studied the Bible and were now just relaxing. We shut the door behind us and before we knew it our hands started wandering. His touch got me, I did not realize when I reciprocated the touch and the touches became more intense. We became our movie and kissed! It was a beautiful and passionate kiss and it was my first, but I honestly wished that we had saved it for our wedding day.

After that episode, we learnt our lesson. One of us tried to be strong whenever the other was weak. I have shared this because despite our boundaries and spiritual strength, we still fell short! Now, imagine if there were no boundaries?

Please set boundaries and do your best, with the grace of God, to stick to it.

His secondary love language was quality time, although it is now his primary love language. This language was a bit challenging for me. I love quality time too, but I was very busy and he didn't like excuses. He could talk with me around the clock and I appreciated it, but sometimes I just needed "me time". I had assignments to do, exams to study for, and I was an executive member in the fellowship in medical school, so I was very busy. I had to apportion time for our relationship out of my busy schedule. Quality time to Samuel meant replying to his emails and sending sweet emails to him before he woke up so he wakes up to read something wonderful from me. This always made his day and he was usually disappointed whenever I didn't do this, for whatever reason. After a lot of struggle, I was able to strike a balance and we pulled through.

He also learnt my love language. It used to be Acts of service and he promised to assist me with house chores when we get married and help me whenever I needed it. Honestly, he has been very amazing with the chores at home. There is nothing that he cannot do! From washing dishes to cooking meals, to cleaning the house including the bathroom and toilet, to bathing the kids and dressing them up, just name it! He assists with everything! He does not make me feel like this job is a woman's job or a wife's job. He is the sweetest husband ever and I am extremely blessed to have him.

He spoke my primary love language to me during my project in medical school. He helped proofread my project and sorted out my references. I was very grateful to him for this. Whenever I had any technical or IT issues, I consulted him to assist me with troubleshooting and he always came to my rescue. Now, my primary love language is quality time and this is so helpful for both of us in marriage because we enjoy spending time with each other.

I will just mention briefly the other love languages. Words of affirmation – those who have this language like people to sing their praises. They feel loved when you compliment them, when you commend them, when you tell them verbally how much they mean to you. If your partner enjoys this, please, it is important that you learn it and speak it often. Don't say, "She knows that I love her, so I don't need to say it all the time". This is a very big mistake. She needs to hear it all the time, so continue to reassure her. This makes her happy and makes you happy as well.

Receiving gifts is the last one. It does not have to be an expensive gift. When you do this, your partner feels that you are thinking about him/her and they are on your mind. It means a lot to those who have this as their primary love language.

Don't just know your partner's love language, it is important for you to ask the other person how they would like you to speak it to them and vice versa so you both are making each other happy.

The fact that we read this book made us aware of each other's love language and brought us even closer together. I would counsel that you both read books together, or if reading different books that you share what you have learnt with each other. If you or your partner do not have the time to sit down and read, a good option is to listen to audio books. Many books are now in audio format, and you can listen to them while taking a walk, driving, on the bus, in the train, etc. You can also listen to podcasts on Christian relationships. Download them and learn. Apart from bonding, it is also an opportunity for you both to grow and learn about marriage and relationships. It broadens your view on how you see things. Videos are another alternative. There are thousands of relationship messages on YouTube. I am an ardent listener to the late Myles Munroe's messages. His relationship messages are fantastic. I encourage you to listen to them too. You should not have any excuse not to invest into your relationship.

Another fun thing we engaged in was exchanging gifts. We surprised each other with gifts and love letters. I bought this beautiful roll of fancy paper with a customised envelope from a gift shop. I would write romantic words to express how much I love him and how much I can't wait for us to be together. I always made sure to let him know that I was blessed to have him. My letter always went with a gift, no matter how small. Sometimes I bought him a belt, sometimes a book – he reads a lot. Other times it was perfumes, wristwatches, or shirts. He would be so surprised to receive them and was very glad I did these things. Reading something written by me meant a lot to my Sweetheart. He also did the same for me. He spoilt me a lot with all sorts of beautiful gifts! I believe that giving should be both ways and not one sided. Don't always be the one to receive all the time, it is important to go out of your way to give to the other person no matter how little. I wasn't working so I had to save from my pocket money just to make him happy.

Apart from our surprise gifts and letters, for us there were three major times of the year where we usually exchanged gifts. Our birthdays, Valentine's day and Christmas. We made sacrifices and went outside of our comfort zones to achieve this. For me, in order to ensure his birthday gift got to him on time I made plans to buy it early enough and send it via courier, about 4-6 weeks (it usually took this long to be delivered), before his birthday to ensure it arrived the week of his birthday at the latest. It was a lot of hassle but knowing how much this meant to him and the joy it would bring to his heart always made me go all the way to please him. He did the same for me.

I remember the last Valentine's Day we celebrated before we were married. He had gotten in touch with my closest female friend and contacted a company in Lagos, Nigeria that sold and delivered beautiful Valentine's gifts. I was very surprised when all the gifts and flowers arrived at my room. I thought they belonged to one of my roommates even though they were on my bed. I could not believe it when I was told they all belonged to me because I never expected him to go to that extent to pleasantly surprise me. In the past, he sometimes sent money through my friend to buy me stuff, but this exceeded my wildest imagination. Samuel is very romantic, and I love him for this and more! This is another reason why your relationship should not be secret. Samuel knew my closest friend, so he had her number and was able to plan everything with her in order to make me happy.

If you are a guy reading this, do your best to blow her mind. Many women love surprises. They want you to show that you love them, especially when you are far away; you have to prove it. You see, long distance relationships are challenging, especially when she has friends who are always with their *boos* and she has a boo that is not visible. She has to encourage herself and remain positive. But a *boo* that goes above and beyond to show his love transcends borders pleases her immensely.

I am sure it is the same for guys too. It is not easy at all, but as a lady, your constant showing of affection through gifts would go a long way in sustaining your relationship. You don't have to spend a lot of money, it could be simple things that you could even do yourself, like making a customized key holder that contains your picture or a picture frame with both of your pictures in it, even your picture frame alone is fine to send to him; so he can put it in a strategic place like his room. It is a constant reminder of you in his life, and when other people see such pictures, it speaks volumes. Before

Samuel and I finally met, I used to send him hard copies of my pictures and he would put all of them on the wall of his room. He made a beautiful wall art with all my pictures.

Just give whatever you can afford. Don't break the bank or go borrowing just to please the other person. Don't give a false impression about yourself. Remember, be honest with the other person all the time, so don't pretend you have millions in the bank if you are struggling financially. My philosophy is that it is the thought behind the gift that matters, not the gift itself.

While in a long-distance courtship, make sure you take time to visit each other often, no matter how difficult the situation is. Love always finds a way. Don't get married to someone you have not had good physical interactions with. Whenever you have the opportunity to see each other physically, it is important to maximize the time. Go for lunch together, dinner dates, watch movies together, pray together.

After Samuel and I saw each other for the first time in 2010, the next time we saw each other again was not until November 2013. I had just finished my final exams in medical school, while he had just finished his PhD programme. He had saved enough money to help process my visa in order for me to visit New Zealand. We agreed it was important for me to see if I liked the country, since we would soon be living together there as husband and wife. I spent six weeks in New Zealand to see how the country was, the weather, the people, to see and interact with his friends, work colleagues, his church members, pastors and acquaintances.

I did not live with him while I visited; I stayed with his pastor and wife, who have now become our spiritual parents. We did not want to sin against God and desired to keep ourselves pure until marriage.

Visiting Samuel was another opportunity for me to observe him in his element. We had a major argument during my visit. I knew before this that my fiancé was temperamental. We had argued a few times over the phone where he would just hang up on me. However, I experienced the height of his anger and saw his attitude first-hand during my visit.

Honestly, I was very concerned about his behaviour, especially the way he raised his voice and walked out on me during that argument. I'll be honest with you, I had to rethink the whole relationship and asked God and myself if I could deal with this in marriage because that was the reality I was seeing. I made up my mind to accept his weaknesses and strengths and pray for him.

We were planning for our marriage already, but I delayed it by another six months to give myself more time to re-think all my decisions. To God's glory, he is much better today. If you are not convinced that you can deal with your partner's weakness, do not go into marriage expecting them to change because they may not change. If you are going to marry someone, be sure you are able to cope with their weaknesses. If they change, fine, if not, marriage is for better or for worse. It is not a place for experimenting, courtship is for that. So, please don't be under any undue pressure to get married! Even if on the wedding day you find out you have been deceived, please do not feel compelled to go into that marriage because a relationship built on lies cannot stand.

A lady was in a relationship with a guy who had a lot of very close female friends. His fiancée kept talking to him about how she did not approve of his closeness with ladies but he never changed. She ended up getting married to him expecting that he will leave his female friends and cleave only to her since he was now married. After all, that was part of the vow he made at the altar. Unfortunately, this was not the case, she was frustrated and began to consider divorce. I pray this will not be your case. Do not go into marriage with the hope that a person will change after the wedding day.

Realize that people don't change overnight. If you cannot tolerate your partner's bad habit or weakness for the rest of your life, then do not marry him/her.

I will encourage you that, before you get married to him/her, ensure you have spent quality time together physically several times to enable you to thoroughly know the person you are planning to spend the rest of your life with. Don't have a long-distance relationship and then jump into marriage without proper physical interaction, and by this I mean at least six months. This is extremely important.

Chapter 9

Take Your Time

Don't rush into marriage with someone you don't know very well. If a physical relationship takes at least one year of courtship, a long-distance relationship should take at least twice as long! Yes! It is important that you know the person and have interacted properly, and you know what to expect in marriage to avoid unpleasant surprises.

My relationship with Samuel was a five-year relationship. This does not include the time spent getting to know him before we started out.

The mistake many people make is, once they think they like the person and become friends and enter into courtship, they view courtship as the time to start preparing for the wedding. While you prepare for the wedding at some stage during your courtship, it is very essential that you continue to get to know the person thoroughly first, as discussed in the previous chapters and lay a solid foundation for your marriage by preparing for your future before embarking on wedding preparations.

I say this because wedding preparation is quite stressful and comes with lots of excitement at the same time. This could cause you to lose sight of the red flags about the person's attitude. The stress of the wedding plans also put a lot of strain on the couple emotionally, financially, mentally, and physically. Misunderstandings and disagreements often happen because each individual, especially ladies, have their dreams of how they want their wedding to be, which the other person may not see as necessary. Hence, proper knowledge of each other is key prior to getting married.

We planned to have our registry marriage during my first visit to New Zealand. It was important for us to have this in order to get my immigration documents sorted as we already made plans to do the white wedding in six months. Getting married meant that I would be applying as his wife, which was an easier way to get a visa to New Zealand at that time.

We had a quiet registry wedding with our pastors and a few friends in attendance. The deed had been done and we were legally married! I was very excited; my husband was everything I prayed for and more. I got God's blessing on a platter of gold without any stress or influence of mine. I give all glory to God.

Can I just make a note of caution to you at this stage? Do not get married to a person just because you want to leave your country. If that is the case, then you know already that the marriage cannot last and that is tantamount to wickedness. Remember the biblical law that you reap whatever you sow, and the harvest always brings forth more fruit than the seed you planted. Make sure you genuinely love the person you are marrying. Do not get married to someone you have reservations about, or you do not have peace about! It is dangerous! Realize that the wedding will probably last for all of 15 minutes if you go to the registry, but forever is a long time to be miserable! Like I mentioned in the previous chapter, even if you find out something strange on the wedding day that you do not agree with, it is still not too late to back out from the relationship.

Realize that once you get married changing your mind means a divorce, which is a long process and damages you and your emotions. You don't have to go through this if you look properly before you leap. God hates divorce, hence the purpose of this book to guide you thoroughly.

"For the Lord God of Israel says that He hates divorce….". (Mal. 2:16a)

You can begin preparing for your wedding when you both are ready for it. Long distance wedding preparations can be more stressful, especially for the lady, from my experience.

In planning for our white wedding, I had to do almost all of it, as Samuel was away. We had a few misunderstandings as he did not agree with some of the daydreams I had of our wedding, like a 7-tier cake. He wanted us to be very careful about our expenses and I was quite upset. Looking back now, I'm glad we cut our coat according to our cloth. We did not have an exquisite wedding, but we are having an exquisite marriage to God's glory. We did not start our marriage with debts.

I would like to encourage you when planning for your wedding, please do not take out loans for your wedding. Save towards it instead and invite only the number of people you can cater for. Ensure you have enough money for each of you to enjoy the start of your marriage with. Don't start your marriage with financial burdens and struggle; it is not worth it at all. If you can afford a glamorous wedding, that's great; make your dreams come true. If not, you can always have a loud anniversary in a few years when both of you are doing better off financially. I am looking forward to my 10-year anniversary as my husband promised me that he will make my wedding dreams come through. Lack of money in a home causes stress on the couple and on the marriage. Please, don't start out in debt.

Finally, ensure you are going to be together immediately after the wedding. If you both are in the same country, ensure you have resigned if you need to and have found another job in your new location. Ensure there is a stable source of income to cater for you both once you get married. Do not continue your relationship as a long-distance marriage. If you are not yet ready to be together, then do not get married. If you are both in different countries, ensure that visa arrangements for the person migrating has been sorted out and that their visa has been approved. It hurts when the visa is rejected or is delayed, and you are already married but have to leave each other as life has to continue. If you need a legal adviser for the visa processing, please do not hesitate to seek one out and pray for favour with your application.

Samuel and I were really blessed to have my visa granted prior to our traditional marriage and white wedding in Nigeria. We were married on Saturday, 25th

May, 2013, and by the following Monday we were on our way to New Zealand to live together as husband and wife.

Chapter 10

LONG-DISTANCE RELATIONSHIP LOVE STORIES

LOVE BEYOND BORDERS – Between Australia and Nigeria

My name is Destiny King from Australia and I'm married to a wonderful man of God, Kelly King from Nigeria. The story I'm about to share is a peculiar story of two people who chose to look beyond the customs of culture, colour and geographical limitation and decided that building a future together was worth the journey.

We pray our story will inspire, encourage and give you hope to know that, although long-distance relationships may not be everybody's cup of tea, if the right principles and devotion are applied, the relationship may truly work and work well. It carries its weight of challenges, but nothing compares to the foundation built, the endurance and strength you both learn to possess, and the unwavering bond of friendship created.

Here's how our love-story began —

I met my husband in 2013 when a group of friends and I travelled to Lagos, Nigeria for an Annual Ministers' Conference. It was my future husband, King, who assisted our group in finding accommodations for our stay and was a member of the same ministry. He also participated in the conference. Before returning home, we exchanged social media handles and kept in touch online from time to time. I travelled to Nigeria for the program the following three consecutive years, where we'd pass each other in church.

Fast-forward to November 2017. A couple of days before his birthday, which was also during the conference period, I contacted King to help me find accommodations, (mind you this was my first call to him since we met in 2013, but as I was prompted in my spirit to do so, I did) and he agreed to help. I arrived on a Sunday morning in Nigeria. He picked me up from the airport and took me to my hotel to settle down. That same day, he offered to take me out to lunch to a lovely hotel in Victoria Island, Lagos. We went for lunch and spoke for a very long time. Prior to this time, we hardly communicated. Our only contact was my often seeing his Facebook posts preaching the Word of

God or sharing content with similar interests to my own.

I liked how deeply intelligent he was, and the various similarities we had. Yes, we grew up with different cultural backgrounds in different cities and miles apart, yet it made no difference to the good food and good company. After lunch, we went back to the hotel and prayed together for almost 30 minutes, this was phase one of a beautiful journey that was lying ahead.

We kept in touch after I returned to Australia and communicated every day for the next year. We, of course, established a relationship during this period until he popped the big question in November 2018. I travelled to Nigeria again, and in the presence of about forty of our mutual friends, he asked me to be Mrs. King and of course, I said YES!

A long-distance relationship from personal experience is definitely not something people often plan for, and it has challenges of its own. When you love someone, you want to see them whenever you feel like it, you want to spend time together, you want to surprise them at their front door, you want to go out on dates, you want to feel their physical presence.

So you see, the distance may be a geographical limitation right now, but if you deliberately plan and craft a life you can enjoy together, the relationship will thrive. My hubby and I would send love letters to each other, he'd order special cakes and flowers for my birthdays and have them delivered to my house. Although he wasn't physically with me, his presence was certainly felt! It is a great way to keep your relationship burning with romance! We also travelled to visit each other as often as we could throughout our relationship and planned for special holidays. This in turn helped strengthen our bond and commitment.

Most importantly, we kept God at the forefront of our relationship. Hubby and I set aside time weekly to pray, fast and study God's word together (during the latter stage of our relationship, it was almost a daily activity lol). I believe practising this in your relationship will help build a very stable foundation so that during challenges and hardships, your relationship will stand the tests of time. If anyone told me my marriage would have started off in a long-distance relationship, I would have laughed it off and not dared to try, but then here I am, in love, married to a man who was not only in a different country but a man who lived on the other side of the Atlantic Ocean lol! It takes faith, God's grace, endurance and understanding from both sides to make it work.

My advice for those who would like to venture into a long-distance relationship is the importance of preparation; mentally, spiritually and emotionally. I can't promise you it'll be easy. You might wake up in the cold of the night crying because you miss the person you love, or have days wishing things could be a little different, but your preparation will help you both move past those temporary tough times. I mentioned earlier that long distance relationships are not for everybody. Before making the decision, allow God, who orchestrates our paths, to share His guidance and direction. Only He truly knows what's best for you. I trust this will help grant you the best years of your life and not a lifetime of heartache.

And for those in the early stages of your relationship; the journey should begin with honesty. Honesty with yourself and the person you plan to pursue a future with. From the onset, be transparent and clear with one another about your values, insecurities, relevant past and present experiences, expectations and so on. You may not discover everything about a person in the first two or three years together, but the openness allows room for beautiful discoveries and growth in your relationship. Go into the relationship with an open heart, an open mind and a strong will for forgiveness, understanding and love. The bible says faith works by love. For your relationship to succeed these two virtues must work hand in hand, so believe in the best of your person and eventually the best of them you will enjoy!

We trust and pray our union will be an example of hope, faith and perseverance to you and your future endeavours.

Yours Truly,
Kelly and Destiny King

LOVE BEYOND BORDERS – Between USA and Nigeria

When I was in my final year in the University, I got a call from my mom's friend. She is like a mother to me and I have known her since I was very little. She said she wanted to know how I was doing, and then added that she had a nephew in the US (I'm in Nigeria). She said when they were both discussing "marriage", I was the one that came to her mind and she would like us to know each other. She encouraged me to pray about him, and she wasn't forcing him on me. I did pray about him, but I didn't get any specific answer from

God, or so I thought (I know God always speaks to His children).

Months passed, and I forgot about it but about seven months after, I got a message from him and we started talking. I must confess that I fell in love with him almost immediately. We chatted for about two weeks, then he began to call me and after that we spoke every single day and did video calls frequently.

When we first started talking, I told him that the peculiarity of my genotype warrants that I ask of his genotype. I told him that I'm AS, he said he is AC, but before then, I had never heard of such a genotype. He knew we didn't match, but he said he wasn't bothered about it and that we should pray to God about us. If we were meant to be together, genotype wouldn't be a barrier. I was bothered about our genotype, but I had developed a total likeness for him, such that cutting off the relationship at that point did not occur to me. Within me I thought, since he's not bothered about it, then I shouldn't be.

The relationship grew gradually, we were so in love. We talked about marriage a lot and his plans of coming home to see me and my parents. I was already imagining our lives together. He told me he was going to visit Nigeria a few months after we got to talking, and that he couldn't wait to see me. When the month came near, I asked him and he said he wasn't going to make it, that he needed to get some things sorted out. He asked me to be patient and he was going to come few months after. I was cool with it, after all we just got to talking and I didn't want to pressure him.

When the time came again, he didn't come, so I asked him to tell me what exactly was going on. He said he hasn't been to Nigeria since he left, and that he needed to get some things sorted (his citizenship was in the pipeline). He asked me to be patient with him, and that he would come home. About a year and six months after, he got his citizenship. I was really happy for him, mainly because now he would be able to come home (or so I thought). He promised to save up money to come but later started giving some excuses again. Anytime I brought up the issue, he would say I should be patient, that he'd come soon. He was really caring, and I must confess that he is a good man, but the fact that he kept promising and failing to come got to me.

He gradually became cold towards me. At first, he used his job as an excuse, claiming he was busy. Later on, he said he needed some time to pray about us. I was disappointed because that was the second time he said he needed time to pray about us. The first time, I was ready to break up with him because I felt he was playing games and wasn't sure if I was meant for him or not. He came back, pleading that he was sorry and he was just confused. So, the second time I told him I wasn't cut out for that. Praying about us meant we weren't going to talk for weeks until he was done "praying". I was devastated that, after about two years of the relationship, he still wasn't sure if he wanted to be with me. On my part, I was sure I wanted to be with him, and I was at rest. Later on, I found out he was disturbed about our genotypes and was generally confused. I was mad at him for, after two years, becoming bothered about it all of a sudden. He used to be the one telling me not to bother about it.

I was the one who broke up with him because already he had gone extremely cold towards me. He also said it was time for the relationship to end, that he thought he heard God about me but he was wrong. I wept and wept. I felt used, I was really hurt. I wish I would have broken up as soon as I discovered our genotype didn't match. Two years wasted, even though we didn't see each other. Until we broke up, I really loved him with all my heart. Sometimes I still cry when I remember him and how our relationship went. It's been five months now and I'm still healing. I pray I find complete closure.

My kind of long-distance relationship isn't one I would advise anyone to go into. Right now, I can't go into another long-distance relationship.

From my experience, I learnt that as a daughter of God, don't start a relationship with someone if you're not sure that person is God's choice for you. Don't assume you're meant for each other, let God be the one to choose for you, not your brain. Also, let things happen naturally, don't try to force things. Ensure that the relationship isn't one-sided. Make sure the person loves you as much as you love them. Talk about your plans of seeing each other and stick to your plans. In doing this, make sure you aren't putting pressure on each other. Most importantly, put God first!

My advice to anyone who is in or is about to go into a long-distance relationship is:

1. Be very sure you really want to be with the person. Nobody likes to be toyed with, or waste precious time of their lives with the wrong person.

2. Be very open to each other, don't hide your feelings, don't keep secrets from each other.

3. Don't break the line of communication.

4. Always let the person know how much he/she means to you and show it in your actions too. Since you aren't seeing each other often, a high level of commitment is needed to sustain the relationship.

5. Ask for each other's genotype at the start. If you don't match, I advise not to go ahead.

Anonymous, Nigeria.

LOVE BEYOND BORDERS – Between New Zealand and Nigeria

I had always prayed to God for specific things I wanted in my future husband from a young age. Thank God for my mum and an aunt who encouraged me and my sister at that time.

I was quite specific about three main traits I wanted to see in my future husband, and some more. Some of the things I looked for were:

- Love for God: not just merely saying it but the person's action over time.

- Alcohol and smoking- I have strong views against these.

- Sense of direction.

- The kind of support I would get. For example, is the person willing to see me fully maximize my God-given potential or instead convince me to remain stagnant?

- Family- I always prayed not just for the right man, but about my future in laws.

God connected my husband and me through an online writers platform, I wasn't even searching at the time. He had the important traits I was looking for; however, we were based at different states in Nigeria at the time. We saw ourselves a few times before he left the country to study overseas in New Zealand. There were a number of things that lured me to remain in the relationship, a couple of these were: His genuine love for God and how romantic he was (and still is). He wrote me really lovely poems regularly- Oh! How I loved them. He genuinely cared about my wellbeing. He seemed like a true leader- had a vision for his life and was clearly able to lead as the head, if we were to get married. He was very open and frank about everything, I loved that as that is the kind of person I am.

We did go through a number of challenges, as with all relationships, but we both prayed to God about it (our relationship) and were convinced we were for each other. I personally weighed all the pros and cons of getting married to my now husband and I knew we could do it. It has been an amazing nearly six years of marital bliss and I can boldly say I made the right decision. Just like wine, our marriage has gotten even better with time – the road seems much smoother.

Some word of advice, from my perspective:

- Be convinced of the person's love for God: during rough patches in the relationship, God can speak to your spouse even if they are unwilling to listen to you at the time. Of course, over time during marriage, both parties learn more about each other and are able to communicate better.

- Do not assume love is blind: go into a relationship with your eyes and mind wide open.

- Get to know the person and tell them all they should know about you. With the wisdom of God, you'll be able to discern if the person is a cheat, drug addict, drunkard etc. and then decide if you are willing to cope with these things for the rest of your life (I do not mean to be harsh).

- Be ready for marriage yourself. Read lots of books – if reading books isn't a habit you have, cultivate it. Read trusted materials online while you are dating, or even before so you know what to look out for.

- All in all, long-distance relationships are possible, if intended for the right reason (marriage in the long run) and with God as the head.

We wish you all the best.

Myles and Tega Ojabo

LOVE BEYOND BORDERS – Within Nigeria

I was about 18 years when I first entered into a relationship. Although at the time I felt ready and mature enough for a relationship, in retrospect I think I was pressured into it. I shared a room with my cousin at the time and she was in a relationship with John (not his real name), a more mature man. John was in Jos while my cousin and I lived in Ilorin, studying. They seemed inseparable and in love. My cousin kept putting pressure on me to have a boyfriend and that it was better to find a life partner now rather than later when men may be "scarce" and time ticked. She allayed my fears of getting into a relationship too soon, so I eventually agreed to date one of the many guys who wooed me.

Mike (not his real name) was very soft spoken, tall and handsome, had a lot of manners and was very pleasing to the eyes. We were soon in love, but after about two months, he left for Jos and everything seemed fine for a while. Although there were no mobile phones like we have now; we often used telephone booths to make calls while frequently exchanging letters. I did look forward to checking the post office then! Communication wise, I would say we did just fine especially as sending electronic mails soon became popular. This meant we could now chat via Yahoo Messenger, have real time responses, exchange many pictures, pray, and just laugh over everyday issues.

Two years and some months into this relationship, I started to lose my peace over our being together. This was very confusing for me because the more I prayed, the more I felt the need to quit. I found this feeling somewhat embarrassing because I thought to myself: What would be my reason for wanting out? What do I tell his siblings, who had started calling me "Iyawo wa", meaning "Our wife"; and my friends who saw us as a perfect match? Wouldn't I look unserious and unfocused? Moreover, we didn't get into a fight and he kept assuring me of his love and commitment to us. Mike couldn't imagine his future without me. I tried to reassure myself that all was well and remember we had come a long way.

Well, one random morning I sent an email to him telling him I was no longer interested. I recall sending it at about 4 pm on a Monday. At around 9 am on Tuesday, Mike was in my sitting room in Lagos. It seemed unbelievable and I thought I was dreaming. My first instinct was to assume he probably was already in town but didn't care to show up, but I was wrong! On reading my email, his friends put together some money and he took a midnight bus to arrive at Lagos in the morning. Oh, what love, you would say!

Mike went on his knees begging me not to quit, asking me why I had wanted to end it, and that he was willing to make amends where necessary. He seemed genuine, cried and my tears flowed freely but my mind was made up. I apologized profusely to him for wasting his time, but I needed to be free from the burden on my heart to be without a relationship. His siblings and friends called to intervene, but I was adamant.

A week after I broke up with him, I was going through my emails, relieving the old times, and then for some strange reasons I checked his own email. I always had his password but never used it. There was no good reason to do so, especially since we had fallen out, but oh well, I did. I saw in his inbox that he had received emails from a number of girls and one of them even recounted how nice their sexual experience was some two weeks back and she couldn't wait to be back in his arms. Oh! I felt upset and unhappy, but it didn't mean much until I decided to check his sent messages. I needed to see his responses to the emails I had read, I needed to know why girls were sending those messages. What I read left me sad, bitter and betrayed. I felt cheated but I was happy and relieved that I had called it quits with him.

It was then things became clear to me why I didn't have peace anymore and the heartaches God wanted to spare me from. Mike seemed to "love" me and knew he found a treasure in me. He was sincere about wanting to spend the rest of his life with me, but he wanted to have his cake and eat it too. He wanted to have flings here and there and commit to the most treasured one in marriage. He was undeserving of me and would never value me. The journey ahead was such a long one and I needed to get the foundation right, or else the building might not stand no matter how hard I tried.

Sometimes in life, until you take the first step of obedience, as in my case to leave, you won't see or have a definite explanation of what God was doing. I am glad I obeyed, and more glad that I never had sex with him even though there was the temptation to do so. This obviously made it easier for me to heal and move on quickly without any strings attached.

Y.0

LOVE BEYOND BORDERS – Between USA and Nigeria

I'm a young man based in New York, USA and I have been dating a Lagos based girl named Kate (not her real name) for the past five years. We are currently planning our wedding for 2020. After the wedding, we hope Kate will be able to join me in the States, thus making the long-distance experience a thing of the past. Now to our story -

Kate and I have been friends since 2009. We lived in the same area in Lagos and attended the same Roman Catholic Church. She was 14 years while I was 20. I was "Brother Damian" to her, and she was "my baby" to me. In other words, it started off as a big brother, baby sister kind of friendship. Little did she know the big brother had plans. lol.

I moved to New York in 2012 while she remained in Lagos. On moving to New York, we still maintained the friendship. A week never passed without us talking. Once a week communication became three days a week, then I started seeing myself not allowing a day to go by without checking up on her (thanks to WhatsApp and Facebook messenger which made communication easier).

I decided to take our friendship to the relationship level during her first year in the University. After she gained admission, I was still seeing her as "my baby". However, as we continued talking, I realized she was gradually growing into a young beautiful lady and other guys were beginning to show interest. That was the moment I thought it was time to take my chance to avoid "had I known".

In 2014, during a long phone conversation from New York, I told her I was interested in her and asked if we could begin to date. She didn't respond immediately, but later agreed to my request. Her response marked the "official" beginning of our long-distance relationship. It took her a long time and several corrections to stop adding the "brother" to my name. She eventually stopped and began to see me more as a partner and less as a big brother.

Our dating relationship has been a bittersweet experience. Before 2014, while we were still friends, we hardly quarrelled or raised our voices at each other. However, the moment we started dating in 2014, a week never passed without us quarrelling. We quarrelled over even the slightest things and sometimes spent days without talking to each other, waiting to see which one of us would be the first to break the silence. I can't remember how many times I called off the relationship, claiming that the long-distance thing wasn't working. But each time, I crawled back into the relationship.

With the quarrels and hassles getting intense, we had to have an honest conversation about it, and part of our resolve was to ensure that the day would never end without us trashing the issues that arose that day. Therefore, we avoided going to sleep without us dealing with issues, and we never went to sleep bearing a grudge. This helped us greatly and was critical in building and maintaining a successful relationship.

She became my best friend and confidant. We talked about everything, knew each other's schedule, and we could guess rightly where each other would be at every point in time. She was interested in my growth and welfare the same way I was interested in hers.

When I started making some money, I began to visit Nigeria for few weeks every year. Since 2016, we have been seeing each other for about two weeks annually. Thanks to family, events were organized back home that made for a good excuse to visit Nigeria, even though my heart knew I was visiting to see Kate.

Exchanging material gifts were also not left out in our relationship despite the distance. At various times, I organized with her siblings to get her a surprise cake and gifts, and she did the same for me through family and friends coming from Nigeria to the States. I also had her account details saved on my phone and I surprised her with a credit alert occasionally.

Kate was no stranger to my family and friends, as she was my go-to person in the time of errands and needs. Anytime I sent stuff for my family or friends, she was the point of contact and intermediary. Anytime I needed things to get to me through a family or friend visiting the States, it was her job to ensure it gets to the person. There was nothing to hide. I wasn't a stranger to her family, and I bonded with her parents and siblings, checking up on them every now and then.

In summary, the key to a successful long-distance relationship from my experience is for each party to date with a purpose. Once a purpose is defined, all the actions, words and emotions from the relationship will then be geared towards the achievement of that purpose.

Thank you.

Anonymous.

LOVE BEYOND BORDERS – Within Nigeria

I had failed my Advanced level exams unexplainably. I say unexplainably because while I was in school preparing for it, I led the faculty academically and got a commendation. After I wrote the exam, I was happy that the questions for all the papers weren't difficult and was assured I would come out in flying colours. Anyway, I did fail but after much conviction I went back to re-take the exams. I was awaiting the results and was with a family friend in Ilorin when I met this guy.

I had known his dad for a while as he was a TV persona with an amazing personality. His dad had a live programme to be aired on TV one day and invited me to be in the audience. When it was time to go, he sent someone to pick me up and take me over to the Nigerian Television Authority (NTA) studio. I didn't expect him to send someone I didn't know to pick me, but I joined in any way.

I realized during our conversation that he was the first son to this man and was only around for a few days. Needless to say, by the time he picked me up and returned me home we were like long lost friends. We most definitely exchanged phone numbers and promised to stay in touch. He took interest in almost everything I was doing at the time and did his bit in getting helpful information, which led to my getting admission into the University. Frank (not his real name) and I soon became very good friends. He was that sort of friend you could go to anytime. Even if he couldn't solve my problems, he made me feel better just by my sharing them with him. We would spend hours talking and laughing at night when phone call rates were cheaper. I found him very captivating and engaging. I got into University eventually and he visited maybe twice, and we became even closer.

A day came when he told me he wanted to start something definite with the intention of marriage. Although, I told him I needed time to pray over it, I knew in my mind it would be a yes because he has been such a good friend all the while and we had grown so fond of each other. Didn't people often say you should marry your best friend? To me, anyone who passed the test of friendship, which he did, would most likely pass the test of a lifetime.

When I travelled to visit him one time, I remember I was to be put up with his neighbour and friend, a lady. The lady, although happy to have me, said it wasn't necessary to avoid sleeping in the same room. We could still stay in the same room without getting intimate. I could use the bed while he slept on the floor, but we knew better.

We were hardly together in the course of our six year courtship as he had to work far away in Adamawa state while I was in Lagos. It was nevertheless a successful relationship. One of the obvious challenges we had was the distance. We weren't seeing each other enough. Absence, they say, makes the heart grow fonder, but if care is not taken it can also make the heart grow weary. He was not there during my memorable moments, like my birthdays where some friends would come around. Yet, the one I loved so much won't be there, which for a second made it look like my suitors seemed more "serious".

There were other family outings where I wanted to introduce him to everyone, but he was unable to make it. Hence, I also encountered people who indirectly said I was being foolish. To them I was in an imaginary relationship and it was stupid of me to trust someone who I wasn't seeing all the time. It was also not easy for me to trust him at first, considering my past long-distance relationship which did not go well, but I forged on.

However, we were very transparent with each other and we shared common values and goals. For instance, although we were very attracted to each other physically and the temptation to hug and kiss passionately was strong when we eventually saw each other, because we were clear at the onset that we wanted to wait until marriage there was no pressure from his end to give in. We were able to help each other at our vulnerable moments.

If my hands were wandering too far, for instance, he would take it away. I did the same. We avoided staying alone when visiting and read the same books so we could discuss our opinions. We went for programs on relationship and marriage whenever he was around and tried to make quality time since we had no quantity time. Again, we weren't dating or trying to check out if the relationship would work, remember we built friendship first and were willing to make it work.

We have been married for eight years now and been blessed with three beautiful children, and we have no iota of regrets whatsoever. I would be sincere in saying that my expectations of him have been exceeded. We are not perfect but have been able to take advantage of our differences and learn from our mistakes.

I would advise long distance relationships, provided the two people are being real. No one should try to impress the other. Also, it may be expensive, but it is worth committing funds to exploring all the modern channels of communication so you go through the day together with a few messages here and there and calls. You should also connect with his or her friends. I mean, do not be isolated from others. People around him or her are able to give valid testimonies of this person or vouch for his character since you are miles apart. I would also say that there should be a fifth and sixth sense to caution you if something is no longer right, and don't hang on out of pity, thinking you have wasted your time. Be careful of when and whom you tell about your distance relationship. Not many are open to this and they may discourage you too early or plant seeds of distrust. Finally, I believe in prayer. It works by ordering your steps to come to the right one for you.

Y.O

I am sure you learnt a lot of lessons from those who shared their stories. A long-distance relationship is very possible if it is built on the right foundation and for the right purpose. I wish you all of God's best as I pray that you meet the right person for you in Jesus' name. Amen.

LET'S CONNECT

I have some free materials for you. Connect with me on social media and be inspired as I write.

Follow me on Facebook
Facebook.com/oluwamayowa
Follow me on Instagram **@dudushewa01**
My blog – **dudushewainspires.com**
Email me on dudushewainspires@gmail.com for relationship mentoring
Book me to speak at your event/relationship seminar – dudushewainspires@gmail.com

About the Author

Blessing Oluwamayowa Ekundayo is a Nigerian-born New Zealander, christian, wife, mother, writer, blogger, relationship coach, and medical doctor. She mentors young ladies who desire to build godly relationships.

She met her husband, **Dr Samuel Ekundayo** online and they have been married for six years, fulfilling the call of God upon their lives together. Their marriage is blessed with two handsome and energetic boys, Oluwasemiloore and Oluwaferanmi Ekundayo.

Made in United States
North Haven, CT
10 December 2021